Beginning French

Beginning French

A MEMOIR

by les Américains

BEGINNING FRENCH

Lessons from a Stone Farmhouse

Visit **www.beginningfrench.com** for new stories, recipes,
updates, and online book club visits.

Keep up with *les Américains* on Twitter **@beginningfrench**

Cover design: Marty Neumeier
Design production: Irene Hoffman
Illustrations: Anthony Smith
Editing: Elizabeth Welch

ISBN 978-0-9974102-0-4

For Sara

Contents

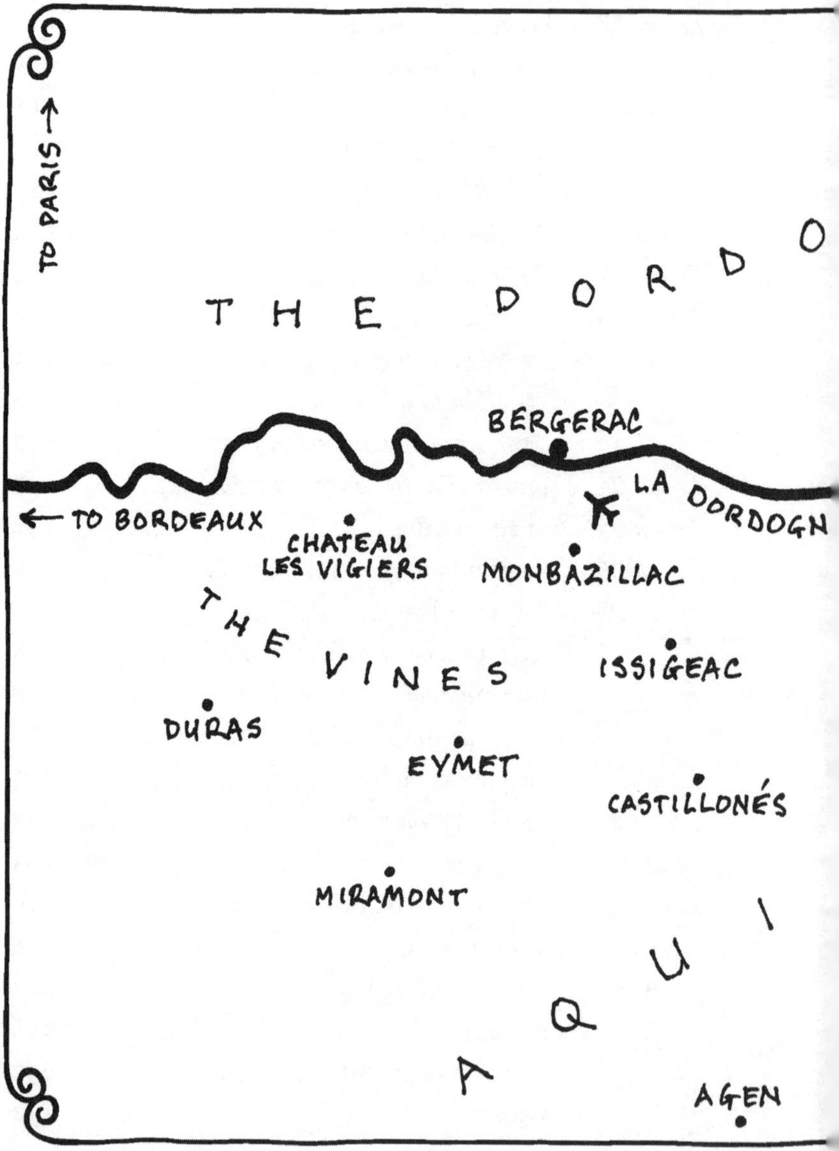
TO PARIS →
THE DORDO
BERGERAC
LA DORDOGN
← TO BORDEAUX
CHATEAU LES VIGIERS
MONBAZILLAC
THE VINES
ISSIGEAC
DURAS
EYMET
CASTILLONÉS
MIRAMONT
AQUI
AGEN

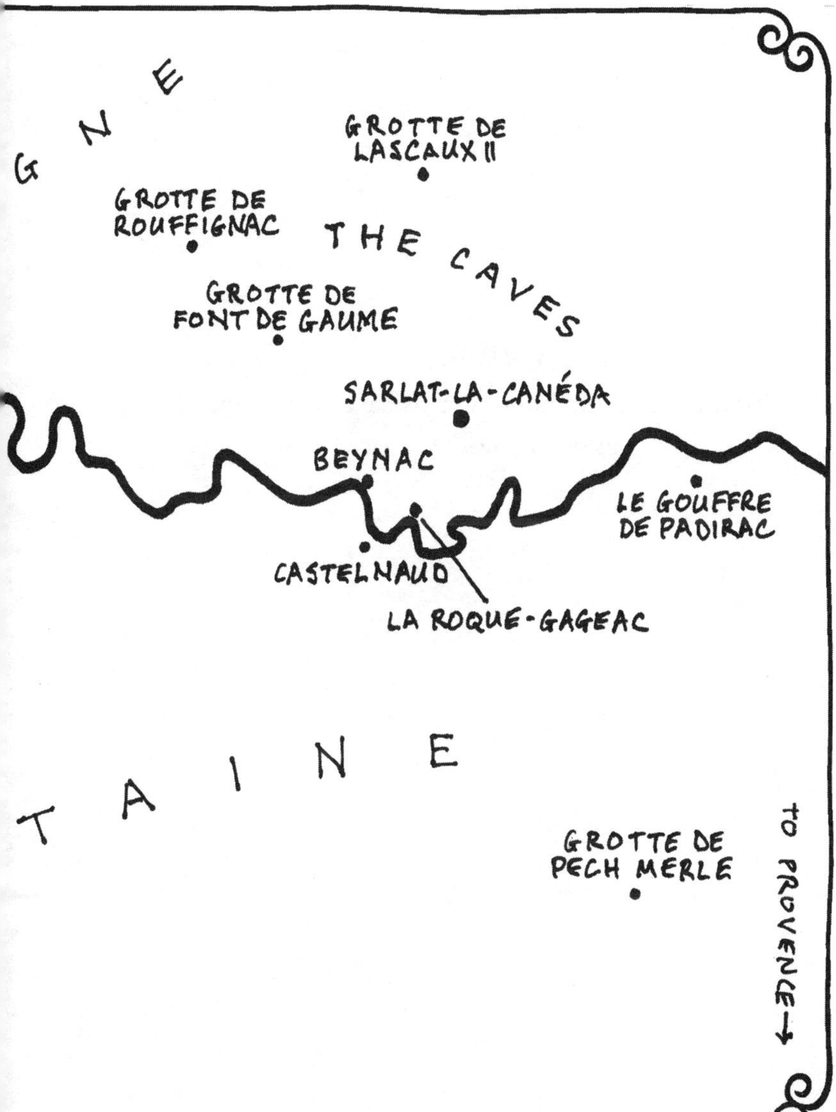

G N E
GROTTE DE LASCAUX II
GROTTE DE ROUFFIGNAC
THE CAVES
GROTTE DE FONT DE GAUME
SARLAT-LA-CANÉDA
BEYNAC
LE GOUFFRE DE PADIRAC
CASTELNAUD
LA ROQUE-GAGEAC
T A I N E
GROTTE DE PECH MERLE
TO PROVENCE →

Authors' Note
Certain names and minor details have been changed
in the interest of privacy

Prologue

THE COUPLE UNLOCKS the French doors and walks onto the stone terrace. Their bodies are stiff, achy, jetlagged. They've just endured the 27-hour ritual in which they drag heavy bags from house to car, car to shuttle, shuttle to plane, plane to plane, plane to taxi, taxi to train, train to car, and car to old stone house—the house that waits patiently all autumn, winter, and spring. They collapse on wicker chairs and stare into the distance. The air is warm. The first stars make their shy appearance.

The woman gets up, her chair creaking. She disappears into the house and returns with a bottle of pale rosé, sets one glass here, one there.

After a long pause, she says: "I'm not sure I can do this anymore."

The man nods. "It's impossible."

They sit, taking small sips as the stars grow bolder and more numerous. A bat zigzags through wooden columns that strain to support a roof heavy with old tiles. The breeze carries the scent of burning vines.

"Of course," the woman says, "I always say that. Then we get here, we come out onto the terrace, and I remember why."

The man turns his head.

"You know—why we do it," she says. "Why we pack up our clothes, our computers, the dogs, everything. Why we close up our house in California and hire strangers to watch over it."

"Why do we?"

"Because of *this*," she says, with an inclusive gesture. "This landscape. This fragrance. This view. As soon as we get here I start to forget all the effort and pain. And then I never want to leave."

The man raises his eyebrows.

"I think we should write a book about this," she says. "I think we should write a book about this part of France, about our friends, our neighbors, about Sara, this house, about learning French. About *this*."

They gaze across the field. A light goes on in the next hamlet over. The sky has become a sea of stars. The Milky Way is the heavenly wake of some huge ocean liner, passing silently millions of miles overhead.

"*Both* of us?" says the man.

"Why not?"

"How can two people write a book?"

The woman drains her glass and places it on the table.

"Same way we do everything," she says, her smile a miniature Milky Way. "You drive and I'll navigate."

He reaches for her hand. They laugh. They walk into the house, where the jetlag and the wine and the fragrance of the night overtake them.

———

FOR THE RECORD, my name is Marty and my wife is Eileen. We're Americans. But here's the thing: if we could introduce ourselves to all of our 320 million neighbors in all of our 50 states, no one would call us Americans. We would simply be Marty and Eileen. Yet in this part of France, no one would call us anything but *les Américains*. Why? Because there are no others. We've looked.

Aside from the French, we see quite a few English. In the summer we hear a smattering of Dutch. While the Dutch may simply be taking advantage of the cheap flights out of Rotterdam, the Brits have a historic claim on the place. They lost it in the Hundred Years' War. And now, six hundred years later, it's as if they're quietly buying it back, bit by bit, hoping no one will notice.

But that doesn't explain why *we're* here, *les Américains*. Or why we traded our life savings for a second house in a part of the world we'd never heard of. We have no historic ties to France, no family members living in the "old country," no vivid memories of cycling through the ripening vines during our gap year. More to the point, we can't just "pop down" like our British friends. We have to slog 7,000 miles through nine time zones and five types of transportation to get here.

No. The reason we ended up in France is much less obvious. We came by mistake. We thought if we bought a house in France, we would—as night follows day—become French.

Now I know what you're thinking: Wow, these people must be loaded. Who buys a house in France on such a whim?

It wasn't like that. There were no silver spoons in the kitchen drawer. We started our marriage as mere children, barely twenty, already raising a child of our own. To pay the rent I peddled handmade greeting cards from the back of an old Volvo. Eileen fed our little family with food stamps. When the greeting card business failed, I set up shop as a freelance designer. Little by little we built a life—I, designing ads and logos, she, keeping the books and running the house.

For the next twenty years, travel was out of the question. But we kept the idea alive—the idea that someday we might visit a few foreign countries, even learn another language. And maybe, just maybe, if we worked hard enough and spent next to nothing on clothes and cars and meals in restaurants, we could afford to *live* in a foreign country. Why not? It doesn't cost a cent to dream.

Lesson 1

La Rêve

It was october of 2007 when I added the final touches to the lettering on the wall. *La Rêve,* the dream. The ideal name for the ideal stone cottage in France. Three decades of wishing, working, and hoping, and we didn't even have to name it ourselves. It came pre-named by the seller. It was fate. Nothing else could account for it.

The two words, *La Rêve,* glistened on the wall as the paint dried in the fading sunlight. The two curving ribbons of French, so lovingly crafted by my own hand, ended gracefully in a flourish after the final *e*. *E* for Eileen, I thought. I feathered a soft shadow beneath the two words for an extra dash of dimension.

Eileen had volunteered to take care of business back home. My responsibility was to furnish the house, filling it with tables and chairs and beds and fresh paint to prepare it for our first vacation in May. I had three weeks to complete the project before getting back to work in San Francisco. And although a whole afternoon spent on signage might seem like indulgence, I felt I'd earned it.

The kitchen now had cutlery, the salon new drapes. The guest bedroom had new bedding, the master bedroom a deluxe new bed (guaranteed for five years). The bathrooms had fluffy white towels, the terrace a shimmering BBQ. In the garden were two *chaises longues* with cream-colored pads. A metal table with six metal chairs beckoned from the shade of an ash tree. In the salon was a flat-screen TV with a DVD player, a minor-brand music system with two decent speakers, and a couple of custom-built bookcases—authentically distressed by an itinerant Portuguese—to organize all the equipment. And the eat-in kitchen had a repainted farm table with eight newly caned chairs.

What I learned from this experience was that, for someone new to France, the smallest transaction could turn into a *grand cauchemar*—a nightmare of Alice-in-Wonderland proportions.

Take a simple thing like a table.

In France there are traveling antique shows called *brocantes*. These outdoor events are staged several times a year in a number of the larger villages. Scores of sellers haul their goods from village to village, hoping to unload used armoires, tarnished candelabra, pockmarked mirrors, bad paintings *à la* Matisse, and all sorts of furniture grown more expensive with abuse. In my single-minded quest for a kitchen table and chairs, I pointed the car toward the picturesque town of Villeréal.

Ascending the hill I could see the stalls edging the old ramparts. Bargain hunters walked down the street in twos and threes toting newfound treasures. Children trailed after parents, holding a toy or a dog or an ice cream cone melting in the midday sun.

Before I could even park the car I saw it—a painted pine table. Eight cane chairs stood off to the side. I quickly found a space and locked the car, nostrils flaring, pulse racing, irises dilating. My ancient hunting instincts had kicked in. Stay calm, I thought. Move slowly. Don't tip your hand.

The whole enterprise was complicated by my lack of language skills. I glanced down at a tiny cheat sheet shaking in my hand. *Trop haute (too tall), trop petite (too small), trop grande (too big), trop lourde (too heavy),* and *trop chère (too expensive).* Also *Combien pour…? (How much for…?)* and *En avez-vous d'autres? (Do you have others?).* I was ready.

The seller was a heavy bald man with plastic tubes trailing from his nose. I sidled up and pointed to a fake Cézanne.

"Combien pour la peinture?" I wasn't sure if I'd asked "How much is the painting?" or "How much is the paint?"

He pulled a wheeled oxygen tank over to the non-Cézanne, rubbed the stubble on his multiple chins.

"Soixante euros."

Soixante euros is pure conjecture on my part. My ear for French numbers was on a par with a German Shepherd's ear for Shakespeare's sonnets.

"Oh la la," I said with alarm. *"Trop chère, trop chère."* Was it too expensive? Who knows? But the opening move in any

negotiation is the immediate expression of shock.

One of the first things Eileen and I learned in French class was that *oh la la* has a different connotation in France than it does in the foreign imagination. In America we say *oooh la la.* In our interpretation, *oooh la la* is the verbal equivalent of a wolf whistle. As in, *"Oooh la la,* check out that *derrière!"* Or *"Oooh la la,* did you see that *negligée* in the shop window?" In France, *oh la la* means something more like "Oh dear, oh dear," or, in some cases, "Oh, no!" when you happen to drop a dish on the kitchen floor. The phrase is also expandable. You can add extra *la*s, usually in pairs, to express additional shock. *"Oh la la la la"* is appropriate when you pull down the entire sideboard, shattering every piece of dinnerware in the house. The goal in life is to keep the *la*s to a minimum.

I moved vaguely in the direction of The Table, showing nothing more than idle curiosity. *"Et la table?"*

"Deux cent vingt-cinq euros."

Another number beyond my dog-like comprehension. He produced a crumpled business card and jotted on the back: 225 euros. I took the pencil from him, crossed out the 225 and wrote 175. He crossed out the 175 and wrote 200.

"Mesurer?" I took one end of my little yellow plastic measuring tape and he took the other—160 centimeters. The excitement drained from my body. The table was ten inches short. Only six of the eight chairs would fit around it.

"Je suis desolé," I said, consulting my cheat sheet. *"Elle est trop petite."*

He replied, *"Pas de problème."* No problem, there were more tables at his shop in Agen. If I would visit him on Tuesday, he was sure he could find one that would suit my needs.

"Et les chaises?"

He promised there were plenty of chairs. In fact, he was a master caner and would happily re-cane any chairs that I chose. Twenty-five euros each. He took his business card from my hand turned it over.

> M. Achille BABINEAUX
> *Cannage de Chaises*

I followed the map to the address on the card. It was not in Agen, but in a residential area called Pont-du-Casse, an hour south of Bergerac. And it was not a shop, but a tract house. Outside on the lawn a ragged troupe of children were playing a game. They got up and followed me to the door.

"Bonjour!" said their father, dragging his oxygen tank behind him. He extended a fleshy hand, then motioned me to a large garage. He pulled opened the doors, revealing a mass of arms and legs. The entire space was crammed to the rafters with a bewildering array of tables and chairs.

Monsieur Babineaux set to work unstacking the tables. He smoked one cigarette after another, plastic tubes dangling from his nostrils. The man was obese and short of breath, but he was strong. He shuffled hundred-pound tables like they were playing cards.

After half an hour it was clear that none of the tables were the right size.

M. Babineaux was undeterred. He led me into the house and down a dark hallway, chuffing like a steam engine. We emerged into the light of the kitchen to find the rest of the family assembled for dinner. They jumped to attention, napkins still tucked in their shirts, as if a visiting commandant had walked into a roomful of cadets.

There, in the center of the kitchen, was the perfect country table. Chunky, rustic, simple.

He snapped a few orders. His wife, sons, and daughters quickly removed all the dinnerware, glasses, and wine bottles. Within seconds they had the table out of the house and onto the front lawn.

I felt as if I'd just robbed a bank. *"Et les chaises?"* I said.

One week later, a rusty truck rattled past the gates into the courtyard. Out came a table and eight chairs, all painted a sophisticated shade of *gris-bleu.* When the set was placed in the empty kitchen, the house finally looked like a home. I snapped a photo and sent it to Eileen.

"Nice table," she said on the phone. "Was it expensive?"

"It was a steal."

I stepped back from the wall. *La Rêve.* The dream. Beautiful. If you ask my friends, they'll tell you I take a certain pride in my skill with a brush. I was a graphic designer in another life, and lettering was my forte.

A small yellow van came jouncing up the dirt lane, churning white dust as it approached the house. It was "Madame La Poste," the woman who brings the mail. She handed me a few envelopes and looked at the wall.

"*Très jolie,*" she said.

My heart swelled with secret satisfaction. It *is* pretty, isn't it? Eileen will be pleased.

"*Mais, monsieur, c'est Le Rêve, pas La Rêve.*" She tapped her finger on the misspelled article.

"*Le,* not *La?*"

"*Le.*"

"*Oh la la.*"

Eileen Speaks French

TWO YEARS EARLIER we had decided to take a short break from the prosaic day-to-day of Silicon Valley. Nothing against technology, progress, and change-the-world ambition. But there's something, I don't know—vaguely unromantic—about the after-work atmosphere in the land of The Next Big Thing. The trees are lush and green, the sky is blue, and the temperatures are plus-or-minus perfect. But it all feels somehow… beige. As if the color were dialed back five or six degrees—not enough to really notice, just enough to make your soul itch.

We had moved there in 1984, soon after the Apple Macintosh came out. One day Eileen was standing in line at the post office as two ladies waxed poetic about the virtues of our new town.

"Can you imagine living anywhere else but Menlo Park?" said the first lady.

"It's paradise," said the second.

Eileen burst into tears.

We had just come from paradise—Santa Barbara, 300 miles to the south. And while we could certainly look forward to better wages in the silicon mines of the north, we sorely missed the red-tile roofs, the languid tar-scented breezes in the afternoon, the calm turquoise sea at dusk. We spent our first year in Menlo amid stacks of unopened boxes, watching *Local Hero* night after night, salty streams coursing down our cheeks as the young oil executive leaves the Scottish seaside village and returns to his colorless life in Houston, accompanied by the plaintive strains of Mark Knopfler's guitar.

So Paris it would be. Two full weeks in the City of Light with our friends Cris and Gordon Mortensen, who had also moved from Santa Barbara, and under similar duress. Together we signed up for French classes on the assumption that a little French—*un peu*—was better than none at all.

Metal desks scraped against linoleum tiles as twenty-five adults took their seats in a colorless classroom. We had our books in front of us—*French in Action I.* Our teacher, Madame Céline, quickly introduced herself, switched on the TV, and pressed PLAY.

"Bonjour," said Pierre Capretz, the on-screen mastermind of the series. *"Moi, je suis le professeur. Et vous? Vous êtes les étudiants."* Got it. He was the professor, we were the students. But what about Madame Céline? So far she spoke only French and we spoke only English.

Pierre then introduced us to the lovely Mireille, her boyfriend Robert, and her younger sister Marie-Laure, who had the habit of sticking the phrase *mystère et boule de gomme*—mystery and bubble gum—into various scenes for comic relief.

While comedy is fine, French is French. After three lessons, more than half the *étudiants* dropped out, including Cris, Gordon, and me. Eileen hung in there, trooper that she is, a dedicated soldier in the French Foreign Legion. Each week she'd come home as if from desert bivouac—dusty, discouraged, and tired to the bone. Each week the same lament. "I can't believe I'm the worst in the class. I'm never the worst in the class."

This is a woman who can quote whole pages of poetry, recite all the kings and queens of England, and identify hundreds of plants by their Latin names. If *she* can't learn French, what hope is there for us mere mortals?

Eventually it came out that we four had been the only beginners in beginning French. Everyone else had taken French I at the very least. Some had taken French II, and a few had taken both courses more than once. Such is the quality of shame that French inspires—no one wants to admit they've failed. There's even a Frenchism for this feeling, which we learned in Lesson Two: *"Ce n'est pas de ma faute."* It's not my fault. My teacher was incompetent. I missed three classes. I'm dyslexic. My cat died.

When the course was over, Madame Céline took Eileen aside. *"C'est de ma faute,"* she said, her face reddening. "I left my sandals in the apartment of some friends near the Bastille. Could you fetch them for me while you're in Paris?" The faintest shadow must have passed over Eileen's face. Madame Céline quickly added, "Don't worry—they speak very good English."

Our train pulled into the Gare du Nord. The platform was teeming with tourists and business people and French families on vacation. Loudspeakers bleated news of trains leaving and trains arriving. The air shimmered with diesel fumes. We stepped out of our compartment into a Monet street scene, an Impressionist movie of a train station going full tilt.

We counted our bags at the taxi stand. Two, four, six, eight—all there. A driver motioned us over to his car and began loading our bags into the back. When most of our luggage was in, he stopped. He yelled something that was cancelled out by street noise. Then he pulled the bags out one by one, and began loading again in a different order.

"Monsieur, votre voiture est trop petite!" Eileen shouted at the top of her voice. Three heads swiveled at once, awestruck by this unexpected mastery of taxi-driver French.

Cris tugged my sleeve. "What did she say?"

"Not sure. Something about 'too small'?"

The driver shrugged, pulled the luggage back out and placed it on the sidewalk for the next taxi. Eileen seemed empowered. I knew what she was thinking: I can really do this, I can speak French. Paris is mine for the taking.

The next morning found us giddy with excitement. Our

first full day promised fine weather and fine adventures. We purchased two bags of croissants from a rue Cler bakery and brought them back to the hotel.

In our room, the phone rang.

"Madame," a voice said to Eileen. It was the hotel manager, a woman with perfectly coiffed hair and a perfectly coiffed poodle who had checked us in the night before. She would like a word with the four of us at the reception desk.

Madame leaned forward, braced her arms on the counter and rasped in a loud whisper. "You do not come to my hotel and parade your *pâtisseries* in front of the breakfast guests." She indicated a small group of diners behind us. "Unlike you, they have *paid* for their hotel meal."

Apparently, there were different rules in France, and we had just tripped over one. We made apologetic sounds and submissive gestures. We offered to reserve tomorrow's breakfast for the sake of international relations. It was her country, after all. Pointing out the differences between our cultures wouldn't serve much purpose. The best strategy in these cases is to make a mental note and move on.

We turned left outside the hotel and walked down the Avenue de la Motte-Picquet toward the Champ de Mars and the Eiffel Tower.

"Wait!" said Gordon, pointing to a sign. "The Hotel Militaire. Wasn't this our number-two choice?"

"Maybe we should get a business card," said Cris dryly. "In case we need to change hotels."

We pushed through the revolving door and angled towards a birch-paneled reception desk. A tidy man in his forties, wearing a red jacket with gold buttons, stood at attention behind it. I nudged Eileen. "Ask him."

"Avez-vous une carte de visite?" she said. The man turned away, his chin angled up. We looked at each other. She asked again, this time more emphatically. *"Monsieur, s'il vous plaît, avez-vous une carte de visite?"* He turned the other way, avoiding eye contact altogether.

We heard a small noise to our left, where a well-dressed woman stood in an office doorway. She said in perfect English: "Gustave, what is the problem?"

The man leveled the full weight of his grievance at Eileen. "She did not say *bonjour!*"

Years ago my wife and I concocted a remedy for these situations. Now, whenever we have a setback, we have a drink. Miss the plane, have a drink. Get lost, have a drink. Pockets picked, have a drink. The four of us walked over to La Terrasse and each downed a double whiskey—except for Gordon, who doesn't drink.

"I'll have a sparkling water," he said, "Straight up."

That evening the sky over Paris wore a swath of pink. The waiters wore black and we wore the best clothes we'd been able to fit in our suitcases. My brother had made reservations for us at a celebrated Michelin-starred restaurant on the Left

Bank, a birthday present I could hardly wait to open.

The dining room was classic Parisian—a sea of candlelit tables and red velvet banquettes surrounded by mustard-tinted, wood-paneled walls. The day's menu was set between red leather covers, printed on satin paper in two columns of engraved italics. *Pâté en croûte, foie gras de canard confit, escargots en coquille, pavé de saumon d'écosse avec sauce béarnaise, sauté gourmand de ris de veau et jus truffé, soufflé glacé aux agrumes.* The chef was reputed to be one of the best in Paris.

"Avez-vous choisi?" asked the waiter. Around the table he went, answering questions and arranging our dinners. Eileen ordered the filet de Saint-Pierre pôelé with potatoes and garlic.

"Trés bien, madame. Et pour votre entrée?

"Pas d'entrée," she said.

"No entrée?"

"No entrée, *merci."*

He blinked in disbelief. *"C'est tout?"*

He inhaled slowly, turned, and carried the orders back to the kitchen. Within minutes the chef exploded through the doors with the waiter in tow.

"Madame," he said from across the room, leveling a chef's knife at Eileen. "You do not come to a fine restaurant and fail to order a starter!" The man's face was a vibrant red. His eyes glared and his heavy body swayed with testosterone-infused menace. If anyone had been talking, they stopped.

Now, one of the things you need to know about my wife

is that she doesn't abide bullies. She's small, and although she may look like a pushover, she is not. She has a Napoleon complex that would make Napoleon think twice. I've seen her bring large men to tears in a matter of seconds. And now, from the corner of my eye, I watched her tendons stiffen.

First, there was the taxi driver. Then, the hotel manager. Finally, the fiasco with the business card. I could see that the trials of the day had brought her to the brink, and this one had sent her right over.

"Monsieur—" she said, pushing back her chair and pulling herself to her full five-foot-two. "You do not speak to a lady in that way. I am the customer. You are the chef. I will eat what I can, and you will prepare it. *D'accord?"*

Time stopped. Total silence gripped the diners as they glanced nervously around. Then, like the surface of a lake stirred by the wind, a wave of applause began to ripple through the room. Conversation resumed at a furious pitch. Women here and there picked up menus to reconsider their orders. Diners smiled admiringly at the French-speaking American.

"Ce n'est pas de ma faute," she said. *"Je suis petite."*

The chef dropped his arm and sagged back to the kitchen, defeated in the first round by the little American.

Each of us had a bite of Eileen's filet de Saint-Pierre pôelé. It was delicious.

Lesson 3

Un Mal de Tête

THE LATE AFTERNOON was cold in the Place de la Bastille. We looked back at our two weeks in Paris with modest satisfaction. We had checked off most of the items on our list. Musée d'Orsay, Arc de Triomphe, Notre Dame, the Place des Vosges. We had gotten lost in the Louvre, wandered through the marketplace in the rue Mouffetarde, taken in the marionettes at the Jardin de Luxembourg. We had watched soccer from the Eiffel Tower, browsed the shelves at Shakespeare and Company, and stood solemnly before the graves of Degas and Picabia at the Cimitière de Montmarte. As a bonus feature, we'd been treated to Gordon's hilarious imitation of Gene Kelley, singing and dancing with his umbrella outside the Centre Pompidou in a sudden downpour.

And now, the only thing left to do was to collect the sandals of Madame Céline. Our friends wisely elected to stay in their hotel room to pack for the long flight home.

"I'm worried," said Eileen. "What if we get there and the two ladies invite us in?" She looked up imploringly. "We'll be stuck for an hour making polite conversation."

"Well, at least they speak English."

"Let's ask them to meet us at a bar instead of their apartment. We can grab the sandals and leave as soon as we've finished our drinks."

Right, I said, and called the number Madame Céline had given us.

"Allo, c'est Juliette."

Within seconds I realized that Juliette didn't speak English. I asked to talk to Gabrielle. When Gabrielle got on the line, same thing. I handed the phone to Eileen. After some back and forth that included the words *pressée* (in a hurry), *chaussures* (shoes), and *bar* (bar), she handed me the phone.

"It's no use," she said. "We'll have to meet them at their apartment."

"Okay. Let's just get the sandals and go."

Their apartment was on the second floor of a building in the rue Saint-Sabin. A woman in her late forties answered the door.

"Bonsoir!" she said with a big smile. *"Je suis Gabrielle, entrez, entrez!"* She shooed us down a hallway in a hail of rapid-fire French.

"They want us to come in for a drink," Eileen whispered over her shoulder. "We can't say no."

Gabrielle quickly introduced us to her roommate Juliette. We rounded the corner of the salon and saw that the dining table had been decked out as if for a state dinner: gleaming dishes, sparkling glasses, polished silverware, and lighted candles, all arranged with precision on a white tablecloth with neatly pressed napkins. In back of the table were floor-to-ceiling shelves that sagged with old jazz records and brainy-looking books on philosophy, history, and popular science. Soft music played on the stereo and the scent of duck confit floated in from the kitchen. A warming fire flickered quietly on the hearth. We were well and truly stuck.

"Alors," said Gabrielle. *"Parlez-vous français?"*

Eileen replied *un peu* and off we went. Apéritifs were poured, hors d'oeuvres were served, and the conversation veered from language to politics to cooking and music. The pinot noir seem to be supplied from some underground river that was pumped up to the kitchen. Juliette was continuously popping up from the table to fill another carafe. Each course was better than the one before it, but we hardly noticed the food, so intent were we in following the train of conversation. I could barely understand more than a few words here and there, but it didn't stop me from talking. Whether I was speaking French or not is anybody's guess.

Eileen, however, seemed to be holding her own. The ladies were nodding and interrupting and giggling with conspiratorial goodwill whenever she said something new.

I don't think I've ever felt so proud of my wife. Here she was in Paris, after braving two semesters of Adult-Ed French, holding an actual conversation with actual French people.

When last of the Calvados was poured, the roommates got up to look for one more dessert treat. Eileen kicked me under the table.

"You've got to get me out of here. Now." She clutched my arm for emphasis. "I've used up all the words I know, and even some I don't. My head is exploding—*un grand mal de tête.* I'm all Frenched out."

After a few more bites of dessert, we conveyed our gratitude, said our goodbyes, and wobbled to the front door.

"Oh la la!" said Gabrielle, holding up her hand. *"Les sandales!"* She disappeared down the hall and came back with a pair of ordinary white-leather sandals that looked like they'd seen better days. *"Et voilá."*

We swayed down the rue Saint-Sabin with the prized shoes, heading for the Metro station. We had to agree that this night had been the highlight of our trip, and maybe the highlight of our traveling careers. The accepted truth is that Parisians are rude to Americans, and sometimes they are. When you visit their city, they expect you to play by their rules. But how do you explain the generous dollop of hospitality lavished on two strangers who could barely hold a conversation? Gabrielle and Juliette performed a kind of magic trick. They transformed us from outsiders to insiders in the course of a single evening.

As the cold night air began to bring a modicum of sobriety to my synapses, I stopped in my tracks.

"Do you think Madame Céline really wanted these sandals back?"

Lesson 4

Ah, the Country Life

THE FRENCH WILL TELL YOU there are two Frances: Paris, and the 36,500 smaller communes that make up the rest of the country. These two Frances are as different as New York City and the rest of the United States. Before we stepped off the plane in California, we'd already made plans to return with our daughter Sara to sample the *other* France.

Sara had taken French all through grammar school, and in her early twenties she entered the workplace as a chef. She wouldn't say "chef," because a chef is someone who runs a kitchen in a restaurant. But on the basis of cooking skills, she's a chef. Rather than work long hours in the backbreaking crush of a commercial kitchen, she had chosen the more civilized occupation of styling food for magazines. She leapt at the chance to sample the cuisine of the very country in which the word *cuisine* was born.

We set our sights on Provence—Avignon, Arles, Saint-Rémy, and Aix—to breathe the same lavender-scented air that drew Matisse, Cézanne, and Picasso to the Côte d'Azur. That summer Eileen and I arrived at the Avignon train station to a chorus of cicadas so loud that we couldn't hear our own thoughts. It was a scene straight out of a Marcel Pagnol movie.

The next day Sara flew directly from New York to meet us there. *"Bonjour mes parents! Ça va?"* she said upon reaching the hotel, her entire two-week wardrobe in a small pink roll-aboard.

In the span of a single week, the three of us sampled what seemed to be every restaurant in the guidebook. We ate our way from Roussillon straight down to Marseilles. We had one of our best meals in a coastal town to the west of Marseilles, beautiful Cassis, at a sidewalk dive that specializes in fish soup. It was in this hot and arid region of France that we acquired a taste for ice-cold rosé.

When the week was up we piled into the car and headed west to Bergerac—as in Cyrano. According to the guidebook, Cyrano was not actually from Bergerac, but the city fathers weren't above riding his coattails. They had erected a large statue—complete with pointy nose, plumed hat, and knee boots—in the center of the old town.

After six hours of driving, the sun was low in the sky and the landscape had turned green and gold with long purple shadows. Vineyards and wheat farms alternated with clumps of forest, and wide expanses of sunflowers gave off an intense yellow light collected from the long summer day. We had never seen such beautiful farms. There were pale amber and tan colored houses with stone walls and clay tile roofs, with none of the clutter you see on commercial American farms. They were the kind of farms that make you want to take off your shoes so you don't get the fields dirty.

One of those farms, no longer a going concern, belonged to our London friends, Susan and David Stuart. They had invited us to stay for a few days on our way back to Paris. Finding the place was a challenge, though. There were no street signs, just enameled metal pointers to various villages. We had to turn the map several ways to figure out where we were.

"There it is!" cried Sara, gesturing toward a white plaster house with a perfectly trimmed hedge. It was positioned hard against the road. Across from it was a small church built of wheat-colored stone, with a stained-glass window and rough wooden doors that appeared to be permanently locked. Next to the church was a small cemetery.

A stately iron gate guarded the Stuarts' property. Behind the gate was a tidy, white-gravel parking area edged with beds of Queen Elizabeth roses, Munstead lavenders, and thick rosemary bushes. A large willow was visible on the lawn a short distance away, and a white gravel path led to the front door.

David and Susan rushed out, arms spread wide. "Our American friends are here!" cried Susan.

"Come in, come in, you darlings" said David. "Are you all right? Did you get lost?"

If you look up *gracious* in Google Images, a picture of the Stuarts pops up. One of our most fervent wishes is to someday be half the hosts that David and Susan are. They handed out drinks, gave us a quick tour of the house, and whisked us off to our rooms to freshen up for dinner.

The next morning they drove us to Miramont, a nearby village with a lively farmer's market. Like many villages in southwest France, Miramont is a *bastide*, a fortified town laid out on a grid. In the center of the grid is a square that serves as the village marketplace. Between 1222 and 1372, nearly 700 bastides were built in the south of France with the intention of colonizing the wilderness. Now they attract tourists and foodies to their central squares with stalls selling hard goods and farm-fresh produce.

I was riffling through a pile of gorgeous patchwork quilts. Eileen rushed over. "You've got to see this," she said, leading me by the hand to an arcade with long tables. Spaced evenly on the tables, in perfect rows, were various heads of lettuce— light green, dark green, pale yellow, multi-hued, curly-edged, loose-leaf. "They look like bridal bouquets!" She scooped one up in her hands and held it out. "Please?" I paid the farmer and we placed the lettuce gently into a plastic sack.

Across the square, David and Susan were buying ingredients for dinner. Sara wandered through the maze of stalls, marveling at the freshness and variety of the food in rural France. It's one thing to see a village on a map. It's another to smell the mussels simmering in the pot, to taste the subtle differences among cheeses, to hear the music of accordion and guitar, to walk on cobbled streets with half-timbered houses leaning out over your head. On the map a village is just a village. When you're standing in the middle of one, you realize that this is a *particular* village, with a *particular* atmosphere and a *particular* magic.

"David, how many really nice villages do you have around here?" I asked.

"Oh, probably dozens within twenty miles or so. Eymet and Duras are especially nice, and so are Issigeac and Castillones. But this village is *our* village."

That night we sat out on the terrace, eating roast lamb and drinking Pecharmant, a local *vin rouge*. We watched the sun rake across the fringed surface of the cornfield that walled the Stuarts' property. A chicken wandered through the hedge and pecked its way across the lawn.

"David," said Susan, "tell everyone how we met our neighbor, Madame Rustand."

"Ah, yes, our introduction to the country life," said David.

The corners of Eileen's mouth turned up. She leaned forward.

"Madame Rustand," he said. "She's very poor, like a lot of people around here. She keeps her own vegetable garden, and some rabbits, ducks, and chickens."

A second chicken made its entrance, hedge right, as if on cue.

"We thought we should do the neighborly thing—you

know, go over and introduce ourselves. She was standing there, in her apron and baggy stockings, a chicken under one arm. The hand of the other arm was turning it into an ex-chicken."

Horrified, I shot a glance at Eileen.

"She wiped the blood on her apron," he continued, "and stuck out her hand for us to shake."

Eileen shrugged as if to say, "Well, that's rural France."

"Then what?" I said.

"Then we were neighbors. She began coming through the hedge every few days to bring us eggs."

"Of course, she doesn't speak English," said Susan. "And my French isn't that great. So we communicate mostly with smiles and gestures." Susan mimed a conversation with Madame Rustand. "Every once in a while we insert a *quel dommage*—what a pity—or an *oh la la* to keep up our end of the conversation."

"Who else lives in the neighborhood?" I asked.

"On the other side we have Monsieur Guenot, who takes care of the pool. He appears out of thin air and gives us a wave when he comes over to work. He doesn't speak English either, so when we need to talk I bring a dictionary, and David brings a sketchbook to make drawings."

"What about carpentry and odd jobs and like that?"

"Monsieur Poulet—"

"Poulet?" I interrupted. "Mr. Chicken?"

"Exactly, Mr. Chicken. A nice man who does little bits of

carpentry and fixes things for us. He was the one you saw this afternoon, painting the back of the house."

The back of the house is really the front, as it has the more impressive façade. Its French doors and shutter-flanked windows face out over the fields to the distant hills. I had remarked on how tall the house looked with a man perched so high up on such a thin ladder.

"Then we have Monsieur and Madame Chouinard who take care of the garden, and Mrs. Carey from Bristol who does the housekeeping."

"It sounds like a well-oiled machine," I said.

"We were just lucky," said Susan. "Most of our helpers came with the house."

The five of us savored our blackberry crumble with a sense of camaraderie and a shared belief in the goodness of life. We capped off dinner with a glass of pale gold Beaume de Venise and called it a night.

Two days later, when we got in the car and headed toward Paris, Sara and I looked at each other with the exact same thought.

"*We* could be French," said Sara.

"What?" Eileen said. "I thought you wanted to be Italian!"

"No, FRENCH!" we cried in unison.

Lesson 5

Pins on a Map

A YEAR LATER I was sticking pins into Michelin map number 524—the Aquitaine, a 16,000-square-mile region in the lower-left corner of France. I had mounted the map on a sheet of foamcore, and leaned the foamcore against the wall of my study. I stuck a black pin into any village that had an attractive house at a good price, and a blue pin if it had a house with a pool. The map was now bristling with tiny black and blue pins.

Rounding up the houses was a tedious task. In those days the internet didn't offer centralized property listings. You had to ferret them out individually by entering search terms like "house for sale in Sarlat-la-Canéda," or more likely, *"maison à vendre à Sarlat-la-Canéda."* Each agency had its own website—if it had a website at all—and each town had its own agencies. But I was on a mission. It took me about three months to transfer all the possibilities from the various websites to the map.

The pins revealed a clear pattern. They clustered heavily in the northern portion of the Aquitaine, forming a wide belt from east to west along the Dordogne River, the watery backbone of the Dordogne *département*. France is divided into a hundred such departments, not unlike our fifty states. The pins also passed through the top of the Lot-et-Garonne, the department where the Stuarts live.

At the west end of the belt is Bordeaux—let's call it the buckle—where some of the most expensive wines in the world are produced. At the east end is Sarlat, with its fairy-tale castles, rocky cliffs, and prehistoric caves.

To our eyes the Bordeaux landscape seems a bit flat and industrial, and Sarlat, while dramatic and dreamlike, is missing the vineyards we envisioned for our life in France. Between the two ends lay the area around Bergerac, a cozy patchwork of vines, villages, forests, and farms.

Don't get me wrong. You can find beautiful regions all over the south. Provence, a prime example, is famous for its dry, stony, Mediterranean landscape. And the Auvergne-Rhône-Alpes can be proud of its peppery red wines. Its capital city, Lyon, is considered by many to be the gastronomic center of France. But the Aquitaine is unique in that it combines extraordinary beauty with a relaxing serenity, an authentic "Frenchness" that remains unspoiled by tourism and commerce.

We prepared a short list of fifteen properties. David and Susan had offered to act as our scouts while they were in France. They drove out to the houses with various estate agents at the rate of one or two a day, reporting back each evening. Each morning (due to the time difference), we would run to the computer to read about the daily catch.

"What? Three on a scale of ten? No way!" I'd say. "I loved that house!"

"It looked much better in the photo," David would reply. The rooms were too big, or the fittings too cheap, or the neighborhood too odd, or something too something. The ads were fiendishly clever in their ability to hide the one fault that would render the house unlivable.

When all fifteen properties were crossed off the list, the highest mark the Stuarts could muster was a seven out of ten.

"It's workable, but you'd need to rip out the cabinets," David would say. Or the plumbing. Or three or four walls.

It's not that Eileen and I are strangers to renovation. It's just that we'd hoped to start with a completely restored house, given our distance from France and our lack of connections there. Where were the move-in-ready homes?

Sometimes when you're shopping for property, you need to loosen your budget so you can breathe. It's like anything else in life. If you want more, pay more. So I raised our top limit by five percent and went back online. Within seconds— *voilà!*—up popped Le Rêve.

"Farmhouse chic," said the ad. "Completely restored *maison de charme* near Issigeac." Under this headline, magazine-quality photos showed a stone house with a lap pool, a high-ceilinged salon, a stone barn, and a 30-mile view from the terrace. "Only ten minutes from the Bergerac airport," the copy said.

It was also 30 minutes from the Stuarts.

"This one's a nine on a scale of ten," said David. "Better get over here."

In person, the house was just as advertised. If anything, it was all the more charming for being real. The large kitchen had a massive white range and a clay tile floor; the two bathrooms were roomy and up to date; and the master bedroom looked out towards the view through two walls of French doors. There was a large old tree in the courtyard.

The only bothersome feature was the barn—an enormous stone structure that lay unchanged for four centuries, built to house the owners' cows and pigs. The floor was nothing but rubble, and the original cow feeders still had ancient bits of hay in them. Stone walls supported a high roof with heavy wooden beams—the repurposed ribs of a Dordogne wine boat. No question that the space was breathtaking. But why pay extra for a farm building without a farm?

On the way home we felt uneasy. A lot was at stake with this purchase, and we knew it was a move we couldn't easily undo. The questions circled round and round in our minds.

Should we buy the house and simply leave the barn as a "relic," the way some people place an antique carriage wheel off to the the side of their driveway? Or should we spend even more money—probably a lot more money—to transform it into habitable space? More realistically, should we just pass on the whole deal and start over?

Lesson 5 : Pins on a Map

Three days went by. I logged onto the computer to see if I could find one or two more pins for the map. There in the inbox was an email from Sara.

Lesson 6

To Buy or Not to Buy

Mes parents,

I know you're on the fence about the house, but here are four good reasons to buy it:

1. I looked up that gorgeous oven/ventilation system on the internet. It costs close to $20K. I don't know what models the dishwasher and refrigerator are, but Miele products are fabulous. If the owner spent that much on the oven, can you imagine how much he sank into the rest of the renovations?

2. The commute is not bad—you can fly into Heathrow and then take a Jetlink bus to Stansted (1hr 20 min) and from there, Ryanair straight to Bergerac for like $60. It's only 10 miles from the airport to Issigeac.

3. Mom, I know you're worried about the money, but it seems to me that this house is about the same price as the others, only a bit smaller

*(less trouble to maintain) and perfectly renovated
(you won't have to put another cent into it!).*
   *4. Finally, I believe you're thinking about
the barn the wrong way. It's the perfect vacation
activity! You can just sit by the pool, outside your
luxuriously renovated country cottage, in perfect
comfort, not doing a lick of work, no pressure,
a glass of rosé in your hand (I'll bring you some
snacks), while you fantasize about what you'll do
with the barn someday. Years of entertainment
right there!*

*xoxo
Sara*

"She has a point," I said. "The barn's a feature, not a flaw. Any object worthy of perpetual fantasy is priceless."

"Now you're reaching," said Eileen. "You can see this is pure rationalization, right? You want the house, so you're ready to grasp at the slimmest of straws. Sara gives you four skinny little reasons, and to you they look like the Pillars of Hercules."

"I thought there were only two Pillars of Hercules."

"You get my drift."

"But don't you agree that the Godin stove is a bonus?" I said to the woman who hates to cook. "It's like subtracting twenty thousand dollars from the price of the house."

"It's more like *adding* twenty thousand dollars to the price of the house."

"But think about Sara. She's a chef. Wouldn't this be a golden opportunity to learn more about French cuisine?"

"Well, I don't think—"

"We hardly ever see Sara. Our house in France could be a 'third place,' like Starbucks, where we could meet and have great conversations. It's an investment in *family*."

"Like Starbucks?"

"You know. Starbucks is supposed to be a neutral third place where people can meet and discuss deep thoughts."

Eileen narrowed her eyes with a look that said *Don't give me that marketing hoohah. I'm not one of your workshop students.* "Who's going to clean the place while we're there? Who'll do the dishes? Vacuum the floors? Make the beds? 'International Laundry Consultant' isn't a title I want on my résumé."

I looked down sheepishly. "Of course, Sara and I will help."

Eileen looked at me. My credibility in this area was seriously lacking. And even if we could hire a housekeeper, we wouldn't. It would destroy our dream of becoming French.

"Okay," she said, "let's start over. Why are we buying a house at all?"

"Because we've always said we wanted to live abroad. I'll probably never retire, and now's as good a time as any."

"And why aren't we renting?"

"Because we agreed that you can't really feel like part of a community if you don't have some skin in the game." Oops, workshop jargon again. "I mean, if you don't put down some roots."

"But why France? You keep telling me you're Italian!"

"I told you I have an Italian *soul*. But Italy doesn't seem very—I don't know—stable. The government is all over the place. Do you really want to own a house in a country that might take your property back at any moment?"

"Where are you getting this?"

"Listen. If you want to live in Europe, you can't just buy a house in *Europe*. You have to buy a house in some country. In some region. In some town. I just feel like the Dordogne is a safer bet than, say, Sicily. Besides," I said, "all the signs are pointing to France."

"Signs."

"Yes, signs. First of all, we took French classes. *You* took them for two semesters. Therefore we must feel some connection to France. Second, you love French literature—French is the language of aesthetics and philosophy and Moliére. Third, Sara loves French cooking, and she already speaks French. Fourth, shall I go on?"

"Can you?"

"Fourth, we already have friends in that part of France who could help us acclimate. Fifth, the seller is an American, which will make it much easier to—"

"Okay, okay, stop."

"It's fate," I said. I could tell she was softening under the steady barrage of masculine logic.

The seller, Dennis Henderson, was adamant. "Whatever you do, don't change a thing until you understand it. For example, those mangers—*mangeoires*—in the barn. They look like dirty old cow troughs, but they're hundreds of years old and make the barn super valuable. You could actually sell them for good money. And the kitchen floor with all those cracked and broken tiles. They're broken because the farmers used to split logs on the floor in front of the stove. That's history, man. Those tiles are irreplaceable."

"What about the drooping roof line of the house?" I asked. "I mean, at some point, will the roof need to be shored up?"

"No, no, no. It's drooping because it follows the original curve of the beam. That ridge beam is made from a single huge tree, and trees aren't perfect. Trust me. Don't change a thing until you've lived there awhile. Look at all the other houses in the area. Develop some respect for the methods, the traditions, the *terroir.*"

This was starting to sound more like an archeological dig than a vacation home. At the same time, there was something that didn't quite add up. The whole back of the house was renovated with a smooth concrete floor instead of poplar planks or clay tiles, and the walls were made of stucco, not stone like the rest of the house.

"That's because the back part is new," he said. "Trying to imitate an old rustic farmhouse would be fake. So I renovated the back part in the style of a new rustic farmhouse, except for the roof, which I was able to keep. It's a mashup of old and *new*, but both sections are true to the building methods of the area, and true to their own times."

"Farmhouse chic," I said.

"Exactement."

When the terms were agreed and all parties had signed on the dotted line, an email arrived from Dennis's real estate attorney. It contained a single-page PDF of a document called a Certificat de Dépôt d'Acte(s) de Société. At the top were a date and ID number, and at the bottom was a government seal with an initial scribbled over it. In the middle it listed the sellers and buyers, and very little else.

"Do you think this is it? The actual deed?" I asked Eileen.

"I don't know. In California we get a thick packet of documents. Maybe the bureaucracy in France is so advanced that all you need is an ID number. The details might be in some big, bureaucratic computer somewhere."

I emailed the attorney. He assured me that one document was all we needed. We bought the house as part of a SCI, a type of property-owning corporation, for which the paperwork was much simpler. "All you have to do is print a copy and save it."

We had our house in France.

Lesson 7

Les Américains en France

"Where do you want the travel books?" I asked Eileen.

"Let me put those away. I don't like the way you do it. You always arrange them by size and color."

"Sure, so they look good and I can find them."

"So they look good and *no one* can find them."

I can see where my system might seem obscure to some people. I turned my attention to the kitchen utensils.

"Let me do that," she said. "The kitchen has to work. There's logic to where each thing goes. You can't just put the spatula next to the bread knife because their handles match."

My moving-in role seemed to be shrinking by the minute. "Well, what *can* I do?"

"Why don't you go out and return the DVD player?"

Oh, yeah. The DVD player. The one I bought during my initial furnishing expedition. It worked for about 45 minutes, then came to a sudden halt in the middle of an action scene. Nothing I did could revive it.

One of the more jarring aspects of rural France is that outside of its many quaint villages, with their 19th-century shops and cobblestone streets, you'll find the biggest big-box stores you'll ever see in your life. They don't have mere supermarkets in rural France. They have *hyper*markets. A single store will contain all the items of a supersized supermarket, plus aisles and aisles of clothing, camping gear, bicycles, gardening tools, major appliances, and stereo equipment. Thankfully, the villages and the giant stores are kept far apart. The giant stores are mostly located on the outskirts of major towns like Bergerac.

It was in one of these stores, Conforama, that I bought the Philips HG-325 DVD player that foundered on its maiden voyage. Conforama, like many big-box stores, asks you to drive your car around to the back to pick up certain items. You make your purchase in a modern, well-lighted store, then go around to a dark, dingy warehouse to sit in a cheap plastic chair and wait for your product to be brought to the front. The warehouse is also where you bring your returns.

The only problem, as I saw it, was that I didn't have the vocabulary to explain why I was returning it. To make matters worse, the heavens had suddenly opened and it was raining cats and dogs *(chats* and *chiens* in French, which are somehow wetter than American cats and dogs). The roadway at the back of the building was two feet deep with water and impassable by car. I parked fifty feet away and waded into the flooded area with the broken Philips player held over my head. When I climbed up the steps to the warehouse, my pants were soaked to the pockets. The clerk behind the desk stared at me without saying a word.

"*Monsieur,*" I said. I straightened my shoulders and placed the dud DVD player on the countertop.

"*Ouais.*"

All of a sudden I was at a loss. How do you explain that an item you purchased months ago worked fine the first time, then simply quit for no reason at all? And how do you take the high ground when your pants are dripping water all over the floor of the waiting room? Where do you start when don't even know the French words for *broken, malfunctioning,* or *defective?*

I mustered the most indignant yet self-assured tone I could fake.

"*Monsieur,*" I said.

"*Ouais.*"

I pointed at the box. Then I pointed at my watch. I poked my finger nine times around the dial at the five-minute marks, indicating 45 minutes. "*Marche, marche, marche, marche, marche, marche, marche, marche.*" Then one final poke on the nine. "*Marche pas.*"

His eyes widened. "*Oh la la,*" he said. He turned around and strode into the back. Returning five seconds later he smacked a brand-new box down on the counter and said, "*Voilà!*"

Eileen had experienced her peak French moment at a fancy dinner with two roommates in their Bastille apartment. I experienced mine—albeit a slightly smaller peak—in the dingy warehouse of Conforama with a broken DVD player and muddy pants. But I did it. I got the job done.

When I pulled up at Le Rêve, the sky had cleared and the view from the courtyard stretched thirty miles into the distance. There was a pink roll-aboard in the salon and a table full of appetizers in the kitchen.

"Mon papa!" said Sara, running up with a hug. "I just got in. I figured you might need some snacks. Especially after going to Conforama and speaking French. Mom's waiting on the terrace. Go outside and I'll bring you some rosé."

The mini-marts in France are a cut above the 7-11s and gas-station shops that dot the highways back home. They sell the usual junk food—chips and cookies and candy bars—but they also sell locally sourced meats, cheeses, bread, fruits, and vegetables, often produced by friends and relatives of the owners. Sara stopped at our nearby "little store" on her way in, grabbing packages of aged jambon sec, duck rillettes, and Cabécou goat cheese. She picked up a fresh baguette and some ripe peaches, tomatoes, basil, and figs.

Before we knew it, spread on the table before us were baguette rounds topped with rillettes; oven-roasted figs wrapped in aged ham and stuffed with goat cheese; a juicy peach, tomato, and basil salad on the side; and a bottle of the world's palest rosé. Eileen topped up our glasses.

We grinned as if we'd just won the lottery. We were together in France, the three of us, enjoying our new vacation home exactly as Sara had described it. The books were put away, the kitchen was organized, the fridge was stocked, and the house was operating smoothly. With the summer still a few months away, our dream house was ready.

◇◇◇

FIGUES RÔTIES AU CHÈVRE ET PANCETTA
Roasted Figs with Goat Cheese, Wrapped in Pancetta

Sara, here. I thought you might like to try one or two of our favorite recipes from the story. This one was inspired by the incredibly juicy ripe figs we found at the shops and markets when we first arrived. The juicier the figs, the more luscious the sauce that forms in the bottom of the pan. *Bon appétit!*

    12 fresh figs
    4–5 ounces soft goat cheese, depending on size of figs
    12 slices pancetta
    12 toothpicks
    1/4 cup balsamic vinegar

1. Heat oven to 425°F degrees. Using a paring knife, cut an "x" one inch deep in the top of each fig. Fill each "x" with a heaping teaspoon of goat cheese. Wrap each fig with pancetta, and secure pancetta with a toothpick.

2. Place in a 9×13-inch baking tray. Roast until pancetta is starting to brown, about 10 minutes.

3. Drizzle with balsamic and continue baking until pancetta is crispy and balsamic has reduced to a syrup, another 5–8 minutes. Serve warm, with pan juices drizzled over the tops.

Serves 4 as an appetizer

SALADE DE TOMATES ET DE PÊCHES
Tomato Peach Salad

In June and July, every corner market in France carries the most delectable peaches, either grown locally or brought up from Spain. The sweetness of the peaches and the acidity of the tomatoes play off each other beautifully, while the red onion adds an elusive *je ne sais quoi.* —*Sara*

1/8 cup very thinly sliced red onion
1 tablespoon sherry vinegar
1 tablespoon extra-virgin olive oil
2 teaspoons honey
3 heirloom tomatoes, cut into 1-inch-thick wedges
1 cup cherry tomatoes, halved
3 ripe peaches, sliced into 1/2-inch-thick wedges
3 tablespoons torn basil leaves
Salt and freshly ground pepper to taste

Combine onion, vinegar, oil, and onion in a bowl, and let sit for 10 minutes to allow flavors to marry. Toss in tomatoes, peaches, and basil; season to taste with salt and pepper. Serve immediately.

Serves 4

☞ Photos and printable versions are at **www.beginningfrench.com**

Lesson 8

French Made Difficult

EILEEN AND I ARE LIGHT TRAVELERS but heavy planners. I'll obsess about schedules. I've never met a hotel, an airline seat, or an activity that I didn't want to book well in advance. My plans are tidy little works of art. Every day is accounted for, down to the hour and the minute. I don't care if we follow the plan or not; I just like having it. Otherwise I live in dread of getting stuck without a room, a flight, or something interesting to do.

Eileen worries about the house. She'll recycle things she's always wanted to get rid of. She'll take items off of counters and put them into cupboards. She'll do the laundry, vacuum the floors, polish the furniture, water the plants. And she frets about leaving the dogs.

"Don't worry, Boodles, next time you'll come," she'll say. "You, too, Bingo. I promise."

She'll make sure they have their dry food, wet food, prescriptions, and freshly cleaned beds. Then she'll write extensive instructions for the house sitter to follow.

Her lists are every bit as detailed as my travel schedules—

maybe more so. She writes them by hand in machine-like italics that look like they're running on tracks. In the pre-computer days people would ask: "Which typeball are you using, the Selectric Pitch-12 Script or Light Italic?"

With only two months to go, we were bouyant with anticipation. We could smell the lavender and feel the warm breezes of the approaching French summer.

On a bright Monday morning in early May, I checked my computer before heading to the office. There was an email from our property managers. The subject line was "Boiler."

> *Dear Marty*
>
> *Over the weekend it was noticed that your boiler has developed a leak. It would be a good idea to replace the boiler and repair the damage as soon as possible. If you like, we can contact the insurance company and have them come out.*
>
> *Sincerely,*
>
> *Margaret Snyder*
> *Dordogne Property Management*

"What is it?" said Eileen.

"It sounds like the water heater in France has sprung a leak. They think the insurance company will pay for it."

"Why not just pay the $300 ourselves?"

Eileen and I are old hands at replacing water heaters, having bought two or three in the last ten years. The running joke in our household is this: Anything that breaks will cost $300.

I glanced at my watch and gave her a quick kiss. "Gotta go. I'll take care of it when I get back tonight."

When I arrived at the office I found another email waiting. This one was from the neighbors up the lane from Le Rêve, Christine and Peter Johnson, who had been friends with Dennis Henderson. We had met them briefly on our last visit.

Dear Marty and Eileen

We obtained your email address from Margaret Snyder at DPM. About two weeks ago we noticed some water coming out of your house and running across the lane. When it didn't stop we called Margaret to alert her to a possible problem. By the time they came, water was pouring out through the stones.

They opened up the house and found that your boiler had exploded. The floor was covered in two inches of water and steam had damaged the walls. I'm afraid most of your furniture is ruined. The steam had been billowing through the house

*for two weeks, so most of the surfaces are badly
mildewed.*

*We're sorry to bring this news to you. We find
this accident surprising, since the boiler was
only three years old. Please let us know if there's
anything we can do to help.*

Christine and Peter Johnson

We quickly cancelled our vacation. Eileen, as usual, was a
trooper. I researched our boiler on the internet and found it
was much more than a water heater. It was an $8,000 piece
of equipment that not only heated our water but the whole
house. I got on the next plane to Bergerac.

Our Guardian Anglos

I STOOD OUTSIDE the wooden gates, the dull buzz of jetlag pressing against the back of my eyes. My misspelled sign was still on the wall: "La Rêve." How symbolic, I thought, pushing open the gates.

In the middle of the courtyard was a haphazard heap of sisal carpets, king-size mattresses, wicker chairs, down pillows, lamp shades, books, art prints, chests of drawers, duvets, blankets, mirrors, drapes, and laundry baskets—a hideous reinterpretation of my three-week shopping spree. A framed picture of our little family lay water-stained and fractured near the bottom. Every stick and fragment was mildew-freckled to a uniform shade of brown. A few of the edges had turned black with mold.

It smelled like death—the death of a dream.

I fumbled with the old iron key in the lock of the kitchen door. It opened and a wave of brown-scented air washed into my nostrils. I saw that the walls, a freshly painted white when we left, were now patterned with mildew spots. The cabinets, the stove, the refrigerator, and the sideboard were streaked with ugly stains.

I opened the door to the laundry room and peered in. The sides of the boiler were bent and hanging, a tangle of pipes and wiring spilling from its guts. The wooden floor was warped and strewn with mops and odd metal parts. A barely audible drip, drip, drip, sounded from somewhere in the room, but I couldn't locate the source. I closed the door.

More items were piled in the master bedroom, perhaps in hopes they could still be salvaged. I removed a metal ladder from the shower, revealing a rust stain on the concrete floor. The glass panes of the French doors had gone nearly opaque with caramel-colored residue.

In the salon, the canvas-covered armchairs were no longer white but multiple shades of umber. Water had condensed on the tongue-and-groove ceiling and was now falling in droplets from the wooden beams. The marble-top writing desk that came with the house was tipped on its side, one of its drawers pulled out and lying capsized on the wet floor. To describe the scene as surreal would be an understatement.

What am I going to tell Eileen? How can I put this so she won't lose all hope? Don't worry, it's not that bad? These things happen all the time? Together we'll get through this? It's only money?

I went back to the kitchen. By some miracle, neither flood nor fog had seriously damaged Monsieur Babineaux's table and chairs. A little paint and polish would probably set them right. *Small favors,* I said to myself.

Just then I felt something welling up inside me, a slowly rising tsunami of self-pity. There was nothing else I could do, so I did it: I sat down, put my head in my hands, and cried. I didn't stop for what might have been five minutes, but felt like an hour.

A sharp knock at the door brought me back.

I wiped a sleeve across my face and stood up. I could see a cloud of white hair shimmering through the dimmed window panes of the kitchen door. It belonged to our expat British neighbor, Christine Johnson. She was holding what appeared to be a pie.

"I thought you might need this," she said, cradling a pale yellow cheesecake covered in paper-thin lemon slices. "I can only imagine what you've been going through. Sod's Law, isn't it? You just finish decorating your house and—poof! Here," she said, handing me the cheesecake. "Peter will be along as soon as he puts away his bits and bobs."

Footsteps crunched in the gravel courtyard. Peter poked his head around the doorjamb.

"How are you getting on, young lad?" he said. "We were concerned. We saw water flowing out across the lane and wondered, *What could be causing that?* We didn't know if we should bother you, so we called your house managers. I must say they took a bloody long time coming out."

I told him I didn't even know we had a boiler.

"Don't worry," said Christine. "It's not so bad. These things happen. You and Eileen will get through it, you'll see."

"It's only money," said Peter with his Yorkshire accent. "Any road, the insurance company will cover it."

"In future," said Christine, "why don't you let Peter and me keep an eye on your place. We'll tell you if we see anything."

"Right," said Peter. "Like a van backing up to the house with four guys and a flashlight!"

We sat together in the mildewed mess of a kitchen for nearly two hours, and I can honestly say that I've never laughed so hard. I agreed to let them watch over the house, just as they had for Dennis. I gave them a spare set of house keys on the condition that we pay them a monthly fee.

"Oh no, no," said Christine. "No. We wouldn't hear of it. What are neighbors for? This is what people do—they help each other."

I spent the night at the Johnsons' house, where the heat was working and the walls had no mildew. They regaled me with stories of the village—the secretive neighbors who grow marijuana, the hardworking farmer who is buying up the fields, the hotel owners who want to retire, the doctor who wants to learn English, the rich family that fights over money, the winemakers who barely get by. They related the saga of Dennis and Le Rêve—how he later bought the adjoining property to keep it from being developed, and then tried to grow grapes on it. The experts said no, the soil wouldn't support it.

They told me their own stories, too, from their days in

England to their decision to live in France. How at first their property was nothing but a mud-covered hill with a ruin of a house and a huge hay shed. Then Dennis came along and bought his own ruin just down the lane. What they saw together was a lot more than a couple of run-down farms in a has-been hamlet. They saw a couple of run-down farms with million-dollar views.

Eileen had said something like that before I got on the plane: "Look, it's just a lot of furniture. Furniture can be ruined, and furniture can be replaced. What can't be ruined and can't be replaced is that view. It's the reason we bought the house. We'll always have it." That's my wife.

The next morning the Johnsons arranged for a flooring specialist to come out and measure Le Rêve for new carpets. The insurance company instructed me to replace all the damaged items and keep the receipts. I thought I might as well start on the floor and work my way up.

Lesson 10

A Ruin with a View

I HEARD THE CLACK of the gate latch and went out to the courtyard to meet the carpeting expert.

"Super VUE!" squealed a young woman in tight jeans and a gauzy blouse. She dropped her sample books and clapped her cheeks. *"Votre petite maison est très, très belle!"* She teetered across the pebbled surface in impossibly high heels.

I suddenly forgot what little French I knew. I was expecting a slightly older, slightly more male carpeting expert, someone who would grunt and scowl and probably work in complete silence. What I got was Marion Cotillard's younger, sexier sister. I rummaged around for a snippet of vocabulary that might resemble French.

"Mais oui," I said, resisting the temptation to add "my little chickadee."

She tossed back her head and stuck out her hand. *"Je m'appelle Jacqueline. Je viens pour mesurer vos chambres."*

Yikes.

"Je m'appelle Marty," I replied. *"Enchanté."*

It must be said—and I'll be the one to say it—I'm a bit

of a flirt when it comes to women. I consider women to be the superior race—superior without having to act superior, which is something you can't say about men. And, unlike many men, I'm not tongue-tied in their presence. But I never expect women to go on the attack as they do in France. Here it seems like a sanctioned sport, a sort of social combat for which American men have had insufficient training.

"*D'abord,*" she said, "*montrez-moi votre chambre.*"

I wasn't sure what I'd heard. It sounded like "take me to your room," but that couldn't be right. She stood facing me with her head tilted, hips forward, slowly pulling out the tab on her tape measure. Pull, snap. Pull, snap.

"Oh, you want to start with the bedroom. *La chambre.*"

"*Ouais.*"

I led her into the house.

"*Oh la la la la,*" she said, looking around. "*C'est horrible! Quelle catastrophe!*"

That much I understood. "*Oui, je sais,*" I said, trying to sound as French as possible. I ventured a small shrug, aiming for a brave note of nonchalance, perhaps a blasé lack of concern.

"*Alors,*" she said, "*vous tirez une extrémité,*" and gave me the tab end of the tape. "*Je vais tirer l'autre.*" She walked over to one side of the room, and I pulled the tape to the other.

Quelle GRANDE CHAMBRE vous avez!" she said. Her blouse fell open slightly as she leaned over to make some notes in a small red book. I suddenly flashed on Little Red

Riding Hood. Was I supposed to be the Big Bad Wolf here? What were we talking about? The size of the room, or something completely different? Clearly, I was out of my league, going hand to hand with a black belt in innuendo.

"Jacqueline," I said, raising one finger like a small white flag. I indicated with a sideways motion of my head that I needed to go outside for a minute.

She gave a slight pout and shrugged. *"Bien sûr."*

I walked out to the terrace and drew a deep breath. What am I doing? I'm middle-aged, I'm married, and I can't actually speak French. My dream of owning a carefree vacation house has just turned to mildewed dust. My wife is holding down the fort in California, and I'm here matching wits with a teenage femme fatale.

It's one thing to be a flirt. It's another thing to lose sight of everything you hold important. My overriding vision in coming to France was to bring our family to a higher plane of happiness.

I stared across the fields and tried to slow my thoughts. The house is a wreck, okay. Our dreams might be in shambles—*are* in shambles. And while I'm spending time here, our business could be tanking back there.

On the other hand, I do have a view. I'm not without a view. Isn't that worth something?

Jacqueline came out when she finished measuring. I walked her to her van and asked her if she got what she needed. She held up the two sample books. *"Quel tapis voulez-vous?"*

"I don't know. *Je sais pas.* Can you—*vous*—pick out the carpets?" I said, pointing to the samples. "Just email me."

She smiled broadly. "I will make you very 'appy."

I packed my bags for California. The other furnishings could wait.

I knew what I had to do.

Lesson 11

Operation Athena

As we say out west, you can put your boots on first or your hat on first. But before that, you have to be a cowboy. It was time to man up.

The plane landed in San Francisco, and Eileen met me with the car outside baggage claim.

"I'm so glad you're back," she said. "I was worried. I really was."

I didn't want to say it, but so was I. My despair had hit rock bottom when I saw the state of the place. I'll never look at that courtyard again without seeing a giant pile of trash that had once been our treasured belongings.

"How bad was it?"

"Pretty bad," I admitted. "But, as you predicted, the view was unharmed. We'll have to start over with most of our stuff, but I think some of the pieces are salvageable. The insurance company is assessing the damage. They'll have a figure in a few weeks."

Eileen drove us home while I gave her the details.

Whenever we have a setback, we have a belt. It's become a

hard and fast rule at our house. So we sat down on the sofa with a stiff glass of rosé and started to talk it over.

"I have an idea," I said.

It was Jacqueline who got me thinking. Women are the answer. They're an undervalued resource in times of great turmoil. We men believe we're the heroes. Our actions can be flashy. We'll run into a burning building or face a hail of bullets. We can lift a car from the legs of a small child or raise the side of a two-story barn. But it's women you want in the foxhole next to you. They'll stay with you when all the men have given up. Better yet, they'll make the effort seem like no effort at all.

I'm not saying that Jacqueline did anything heroic. She couldn't have cared less about some old guy with a busted boiler. She just tried to inject a little fun into a bad situation.

Now it was time to bring in the A team.

I called Margaret at DPM and gave her the responsibility for dealing with the insurance company. It would be her job to meet the assessors at the property, schedule the cleanup jobs, supervise the painters, and sign off on the work sheets. She would manage the carpet company and make sure all the leftover "bits and bobs" were hauled away. The goal was a move-in-ready house.

Next, I scheduled a meeting with Jenna, a young go-getter at the office. With all the time I was spending in France, I needed a strong person to cover for me. During her first six months she'd shown exceptional skill and judgment in handling both clients and employees, and in her last performance review she expressed readiness to take on a larger role. I gave it to her.

Then I called Sara. Sara has her own business in New York, a freelance career styling food for magazines and advertising agencies. She'd cut her teeth working for Martha Stewart at Omnimedia, and with the contacts she made there she struck out on her own. I hoped she could take a break from her busy schedule, even at the risk of losing significant income. I offered to pay for her time if she'd consider it. To my relief, she readily agreed.

Finally, I turned to my trooper. My Athena in blue jeans.

"Sweetie, I think we need to go forward with our trip this summer," I said. "It won't be anything like the vacation we planned. We won't be able to bring the dogs this year. It'll be all work and no play. But I've made some arrangements at the office and Sara can meet us in France and help us plow through the re-buying and re-decorating chores. We'll get it done. Next year will be great."

"You forget," she said, "that was my idea. But nice work anyway."

See what I mean? Women make it look effortless. They can even make you believe you're the hero—for a few minutes. Mark my words, women will one day rule the world.

"Here's what we'll do," she said. "You take care of business with Margaret and the insurance company, and I'll take care of the travel arrangements."

"I think I can handle Margaret and the travel while you're getting the house ready. I'm a man of many talents."

"Not that many," she said.

So began Operation Athena, in which we Americans show the French what we're made of.

We arrived in early July. Along the winding road from the Bergerac airport the vines were leafing out well and the fields of sunflowers were glowing brightly. In France, sunflowers are called *tournesols,* plants that turn toward the sun. Their faces seemed to follow us as we detoured past the postcard village of Issigeac (pronounced *IS-he-Jack),* our nearest market town. We needed to remind ourselves that southwest France is more than autoroutes and big-box stores, even though these were likely to dominate our summer.

We opened the gates at Le Réve. I turned the key in the old lock of the kitchen door. As we entered, we were met by heady odors of fresh paint, fuel oil, and damp stone. In future years the combined fragrance of fuel, stone, and sisal carpets would become an aphrodisiac, a perfume guaranteed to reignite our love of France. But for now the floors were bare, the aromatic sisal not due for another two days.

We looked around. The walls and ceilings had been repainted a soft white. The appliances were gleaming. The dishes were stacked in the glass-fronted cabinets, and the table and chairs looked almost new.

We were surprised to find that the salon still had furniture. The cleanup crew had managed to save the TV cabinet, the bookshelf, and the marble-topped table. Miraculously, most of the electronic equipment was undamaged by the deluge, including my hard-won DVD player. The heavy drapes had been cleaned and rehung over the French doors that led to the courtyard. The only real casualties were the carpeting, the books, and the slipcovers for the four overstuffed chairs.

The guest room was the furthest from the explosion, and therefore had escaped the worst of it. The bed had been ruined, along with the carpeting and some rather expensive framed prints, but the wardrobe and night tables were fine. We'd have to replace the lamps, as well as the towels in the guest bathroom.

The master bedroom was another story.

Bed, gone. Carpet, gone. Drapes, which had softened the look of the wall in back of the bed—gone. The only piece of furniture left in the room was an inexpensive parsons table in the corner. The adjoining bathroom was also empty. The wood-framed mirrors had been tossed, along with eight small wicker baskets that held our bathroom supplies over the sink. The shower floor showed a permanent scar from the rusty metal ladder, but the large bathtub in the corner looked better than ever.

Margaret and the cleanup team had done a good job.

The first order of business was beds. That night we slept at a hotel, and in the morning a truck arrived from Literie 24 with the two king-size beds that I'd ordered by phone. Margaret had lent us some bedding until we had time to buy new pillows, sheets, and duvets.

In the morning we woke to a rosy sunrise that poured through four pairs of French doors. The master bedroom was designed to receive the first light from the east, and though we were tempted to add drapes or shades, we later came to appreciate the stars that twinkled so loudly at night that we couldn't sleep, and the soft pink light that woke us so quietly in the morning.

We were barely dressed when we heard the front gate squeak. It was Jacqueline and the carpet installers.

"They're here!" cried Eileen.

Jacqueline quickly opened the French doors and two men came into the house with a large roll of sisal carpeting. They removed all the furniture from the salon and started pushing the carpet up to the walls. When the salon was covered and the carpet trimmed, they went back to the truck and brought in the two rugs for the bedrooms.

We stood back and admired our new floors. The colors and textures were perfect, even better than the original carpeting. We offered our thanks to the carpeters and said our goodbyes, closing the gates behind them.

"You didn't tell me," said Eileen.

"Tell you what?"

"That Jacqueline is so sexy. She looks like she could be Marion Cotillard's younger sister. What was all that flirting about?"

My face felt hot. Was I flirting? I thought I was just being polite. Can I help it if certain French girls are attracted to older men? I never asked her to call me *chérie*. That was her idea.

Eileen looked me in the eye. "Be careful," she said.

Lesson 12

Lost in Leclerc

No MATTER WHAT your intentions when you go out to buy groceries, you'll end up at Leclerc. It's one of the immutable laws of French life. A smaller market will be closed for lunch. A specialty shop, if open, won't have the other items you need. Another hypermarket will have all the items you need, but you won't be able to find them.

All in all, it's much safer to drive past the other shops and go straight to Leclerc. The name is pronounced *Look-CLARE,* as in "Look, Clare, fourteen brands of pale blue deodorant!" While we've certainly come across other hypermarkets in France—Carrefour, Auchan, and Hyper U, for example— Leclerc is the one that snares us every time.

Sara had flown in the day before, and here she was, already pushing a large plastic shopping cart through the produce aisle. I was a block away in the wine section, puzzling over the various gold-medal, silver-medal, bronze-medal, and best-in-class winners.

Sara is an organized shopper. She'll fill up a yellow sheet with two columns, one for produce and one for packaged goods. She'll tear the sheet down the middle and give me the half with the packaged goods. She shops for the vegetables, meats, and cheeses herself. This is a task that takes a chef's eye. She also gets ideas from what she actually finds in the store, triggering on-the-spot shifts in menu strategy.

Our goal was not just to fill the fridge, but to plug some of the other gaps in the household. For example, we needed a toaster, a food processor, and a set of champagne glasses *(naturellement),* and various hand tools for the kitchen. We also needed a vacuum cleaner, a 50-liter garbage bin, and French movies for the DVD player. All of these items—and many more—can be found within the four massive walls of Leclerc.

We trundled our two super-sized shopping carts piled with food and appliances over to the checkout section. Leclerc has 32 cashier stations, each with a line of shoppers stretching straight across the front aisle into the food section. As a result, any shopper trying to get down the aisle has to ask permission to pass, causing both parties considerable annoyance.

"Obviously, they don't believe in bending the lines," I whispered to Sara.

"I guess they only do straight lines in France."

"What if we start to bend it when we get closer."

"Not sure," she said. "People in France have rules. For example, if you don't put a bar in back of your items on the conveyor belt, the next person will do it for you. And probably give you a look of contempt. Or pity. In the States, it's much more situational. You might skip the whole bar thing if it's obvious where *your* food ends and the *other* person's begins. In the States you'd feel stupid using a bar with nobody else around."

As we got closer we angled our carts slightly out to the right to let other people pass through the aisle. Instead of following suit, the rest of line immediately closed up as if we had opted out. There was no room in the French imagination for a different kind of line. It was straight or nothing.

"Pardon, madame," I said, trying to get back into the line. I knew what she was thinking: *You chose to get out of the line, and now you want to get back in. You should've thought of that before.* She reluctantly backed up, causing the rest of the line to back up, creating a domino effect of apologies.

The rules of the hypermarket also dictate that shoppers bag their own groceries. You either bring your own bag, as we did, or you buy a bag from the cashier. We were bagging like crazy, trying to avoid the further ire of the line, when the cashier halted her work mid-item.

"Vous n'avez pas marqué vos fruits," she said, holding up a bag of pears.

Sara looked puzzled. *"Marqué, marqué.* Oh, no!" she cried. She grabbed the bag and ran back into the store, while the other shoppers traded knowing glances. A few started to whisper. Soon the whole line was whispering and laughing.

We had broken another hard rule of the hypermarket. You have to mark your own produce. You weigh all of your fruits and vegetables on a special machine that spits out a price tag. You stick the price tag on your item before you check out. No exceptions.

"*Américains*," I explained with a shrug. More laughter.

"*Dommage*," said one person. Too bad. The whole line was howling. Sara ran back with the pears all bagged and tagged. The two of us, red-faced and sweating, pushed our carts to the parking lot.

When we got back I called David. "Have you ever been lost in Leclerc?"

Sara believes that a happy occasion can be made happier with a fabulous meal. Conversely, she feels that an unhappy situation can be reversed in exactly the same way. No matter what the question, good food is the answer.

Making dinner with Sara is like a culinary version of *The Music Man*:

> *Cook a little, talk a little, cook a little, talk a little,*
> *eat eat eat, talk a lot, cook a little more...*

She emptied a bag of *moules,* or mussels, into a pot with a little boiling water.

"Dad, when these are steamed open can you put them on a baking sheet?"

"You betcha, sweetheart."

I split the shells and then placed each mussel on one of the halves, spreading them evenly over the sheet. Sara had made a paste of garlic, parsley, softened butter, ground toasted almonds, and breadcrumbs soaked in Bergerac sec. As instructed, I topped each mussel with a spoonful of the paste while Sara got started on a goat cheese soufflé.

"Have you figured out the oven yet?" I said.

She glanced doubtfully at the strange hieroglyphics on the knobs of the Godin.

"MOM!"

Eileen came into the kitchen.

"Mom, can you figure out the oven?"

She looked at the knobs. "This isn't really my area," she said. "Stoves and I are not on speaking terms."

"Can you go online and see?"

Just then all the lights in the house went out. The microwave clunked to a halt. The washing machine and dryer went silent in the laundry room.

"What happened?" I said.

"Too many appliances on," Eileen said, groping around for some matches. She lit a candle and went to look for the flashlight.

"We've got to get the soufflé done," said Sara. She shoved a mixing bowl at me and I started whisking the egg whites into stiff peaks. In the meantime, Sara carried the candle over to the oven. Luckily, the Godin is gas.

"You two keep working," said Eileen, taking the flashlight.

"I'll deal with the electricity."

Sara stared at the arcane symbols on the knobs. "This one has flames shooting in from the top and bottom of a little square. Do you think that's it?" She turned the knob to the flame symbol, and cranked another knob up to 7. "That should be about right for a soufflé."

I shouted in the direction of the salon: "Dennis said if the lights went out, just push the black button in the wooden box."

"What wooden box?" Eileen yelled back.

"On the wall of the salon!"

She came back into the kitchen. "It's not working.

I think we need a drink." She stuck a bottle of bubbly in the freezer.

Sara slid the soufflé into the oven, closed the door gently, and started making a salad.

Out on the terrace, Eileen lit two candles and set the table. She poured a tiny amount of vin de noix into the bottom of three new champagne glasses.

I called the Johnsons on my cell phone and Christine answered. "It's dark over here, too," she said. "Sod's Law. Always happens when you're cooking."

Eileen went back into the darkened kitchen to help Sara. Moments later they came out with platters of food.

"A toast," I said, pouring the wine. "To Sara's beautiful meal—whether we can see it or not."

We touched glasses and tucked in our napkins. The moules

aux amande were heavenly. The salad was tangy and crisp. The soufflé, with a mélange of cheeses from the impressive Leclerc fromage department, was baked to fluffy perfection.

Just as we were finishing, the lights came back on.

"Sod's Law!" cried Eileen and Sara.

MOULES AUX AMANDES
Mussels with Almonds

The nuttiness of toasted almonds magically elevates the briny, slightly musky flavor of mussels to *haute cuisine.* These addictive bites can be made ahead and frozen before baking—they're great to have in your freezer for an impromptu treat with a glass of wine. Just broil the frozen mussels as directed, with a skosh more cooking time. —*Sara*

2-pound bag live mussels
1/2 cup sliced almonds, lightly toasted
1 clove garlic, sliced
1/8 cup flat-leaf parsley leaves
1/2 teaspoon kosher salt, plus more to taste
4 tablespoons unsalted butter, room temperature
3 tablespoons dry white wine
Freshly ground black pepper, to taste
3 tablespoons plain dried breadcrumbs
1 lemon, cut into wedges

1. Heat oven to medium broil. Clean and scrape the mussels under running water, discarding any with cracked shells. Fill a large pot with 3/4 inch of water, and place over medium-high heat. When boiling, add mussels and cover. Cook, stirring once or twice, until all mussels have opened, about 5 minutes.

Using tongs or a slotted spoon, transfer mussels to a bowl to cool. Reserve 1/4 cup of the leftover liquid for the almond butter.

2. Place almonds, garlic, parsley, and salt in a food processor and pulse until coarsely ground. Add butter and pulse until just combined. With processor running, drizzle in wine and reserved mussel broth; process until combined. Adjust seasoning with salt and pepper to taste.

3. Separate the mussel shells, and put each mussel meat on the prettier shell half. Place mussels on a large baking sheet. Cover each mussel with a spoonful of the almond butter. Sprinkle tops with breadcrumbs. Broil until golden, 4–6 minutes. Serve hot with fresh lemon wedges on the side.

Serves 4–6 as an appetizer

SOUFFLÉ AU FROMAGE DE CHÈVRE
Goat Cheese Soufflé

Do you think there's nothing left to eat in the house? Do you have eggs? Do you have a little goat cheese? Then you have the ingredients for one of our favorite lunches. It never ceases to be a thrill taking it out of the oven! Bucheron cheese hits exactly the right note of pungency, but you can achieve the same effect by combining a mild, fresh goat cheese with a stronger, more aged one. —*Sara*

3 tablespoons unsalted butter, plus more for the dish
1/4 cup all-purpose flour
1 cup whole milk or heavy cream, warmed in the
    microwave
Pinch cayenne
Salt and freshly ground pepper, to taste
4 egg yolks
5 ounces Bucheron goat cheese, crumbled
6 egg whites
1 teaspoon fresh thyme leaves, chopped

1. Preheat the oven to 400°F. Butter a 6-cup soufflé dish or an 8-cup gratin dish.

2. Melt butter in a medium saucepan over medium-low heat. When foamy, whisk in the flour, and cook, stirring, for several minutes. Whisk in the milk and stir vigorously until the mixture is smooth and thick, about 8 minutes. Remove from heat. Add cayenne and season with salt and pepper. Beat in the egg yolks one at a time until well blended, then lightly stir in cheese.

3. Beat the egg whites with a pinch of salt until they form firm peaks, then stir one-quarter of them into the base to lighten the mixture. Fold in the rest and transfer to the prepared dish. Bake until golden (about 15 minutes), then cover lightly with foil and continue baking until just a bit wobbly in the center, 12–18 more minutes. Remove, scatter the thyme over the top, and serve immediately.

Serves 4 as a light course with salad

☞ Photos and printable versions are at **www.beginningfrench.com**

Lesson 13

Seven Plagues of Issigeac

ONE OF THE APPLIANCES we bought at Leclerc was an HP Photosmart All-in-One printer. This is a marvelous device. It can print photos, make copies, scan documents, and even send faxes should you ever feel the need. The ink is expensive, but only if you use it to print more than a few recipes, maps, and the travel schedules.

On my first trip to Le Rêve, I had set up a triple-play account with Orange. They offer television, telephone, and internet for only 39 euros a month, about a third of what we pay in the States. I still remember my conversation at the store.

"Parlez-vous anglais?" I said. This phrase is highly recommended for all travelers to rural France. It lets you off the hook from the get-go. It turns the tables so that you're no longer the one who feels like an uneducated nincompoop. Of course, this wouldn't work in rural America. The person behind the counter would simply say, *"No,* I don't speak your Frenchy-French language. Talk English." But in France there's an obligation to appear cultured.

"I can speak a *leetle*," said the sales person.

I told him I needed to wire up my house for everything under the sun, including internet.

"Wiss wiffy?" he asked.

"Wiffy? I don't understand."

"Do you want to connect wissout, um ..." He made a pulling-apart gesture with his two hands, fingers pinched together.

"A wire? Oh, wi-fi! *Oui.*"

I produced a recent electricity bill as a proof of my existence, and off I went, contract in hand.

The printer was now unboxed and sitting on the parsons table in the bedroom. Sara and I followed the setup instructions as closely as we could. We got stuck when we tried to enter the 35-character passphrase from the wi-fi box. This is the code that enables the computer to talk to the wi-fi, which in turn talks to the printer. Nobody was talking to anybody. I reached for the phone and dialed our hamlet's IT department..

"Peter, can you help?"

"Don't touch anything," he said. "I'll be right over."

Peter Johnson is an engineer by profession, largely self-taught. This means he can actually figure out how things work. He sat down at the computer and plowed through all the screens. No luck. He went through the whole process again. Silence. No blinking lights. Nothing. We stared at the wi-fi router. The router stared back. We entered the code more deliberately, calling out the 35 characters one by one, like flight control at Houston's Space Center.

"Seven."

"Seven, check."

"Uppercase *C,* as in Charlie."

"*C,* check."

"Lowercase *b,* as in bravo."

"Lowercase *b,* check."

This time the computer gave us thumbs up. All that was left to do was turn on the printer. I placed a sheet of paper in the document feeder, chose a random recipe from the computer, and pressed START. The printer lurched into action, then immediately stopped.

"Jammed," I said. "I can't believe it. A brand new printer. It's just like that DVD player. What's with the stuff they sell here in France?"

Peter peered into the output slot. "Do you have a torch?"

I brought a flashlight in from the kitchen and slapped it into his hand.

He aimed it into the abyss. "There's something stuck in the rollers. It looks like a frog."

Sara ran into the salon. "Mom, quick! There's a dead frog in the printer!"

It's understood in our household that Eileen is the expert in All Things Nature. Cats, dogs, birds, horses, insects, plants, stars—even frogs, dead or alive—are considered part of her purview. She pointed the flashlight into the slot.

"I see it. It's a tree frog, completely flattened. Oh, poor little thing. I hate it when this happens."

She rummaged through her bathroom bag and came up with a pair of tweezers. Ever so gently, she pulled at one of its froggy legs. A tiny, paper-thin body began to emerge. We watched this delicate operation with intense interest, bringing our faces up close to the printer.

The frog, suddenly released from the rollers, leapt out of the machine as if shot from a gun. For a split second its tiny face looked as large as a monster's. All four humans flew back in unison, shrieking in horror.

"There it goes!" cried Sara.

The frog, now reinflated, was out the door and hopping across the terrace. Before we could catch it, the creature had jumped over the retaining wall and down into the field to safety.

We went back in and restarted the printer. Out came a perfect copy of a recipe for cuisse de grenouille de Provence— sautéed frogs' legs. Really, you can't make this stuff up.

That year was the year of the tree frog. But other years have brought other plagues. We've counted seven so far. As a public service to our future neighbors, we've catalogued them here, along with our personally tested remedies.

1. Tree frogs. Keep them out of the house. They'll go right for your electronics, appliances, and fine antiques. You'll find them squirming around in your shirt pocket or jumping out from the seat cushions when you least expect it. In time, they'll simply hop away, leaving you to wonder what all the fuss was about. They are not suitable for cooking.

2. Snails. These may be suitable for cooking, we don't know. Sara and a friend suffered an orchestrated attack by an endless army of these creatures while staying at Le Rêve by themselves. To hear Sara tell it, they couldn't leave the house without crunching hundreds of these gastropods underfoot. All we can say is, wear shoes. At night, bring a flashlight. And whatever you do, don't leave the windows open. One day they will simply evaporate from the garden like the morning dew.

3. Pine martens. The European pine marten *(Martes martes)* can scrunch himself so flat that he and his family members can slip between your roof tiles and set up house in your attic. This wouldn't be bad except they're nocturnal. They stay up all night rearranging their furniture, then sleep quietly all day. Don't let them. Before you head off to Leclerc, turn up the reggae music to full volume. (Christophe Maé is suitable.) By the time you get back they'll have left in disgust.

4. Flies. These are just ordinary flies, same as you'll find anywhere in the world. But in rural France they act entitled. They labor under the illusion that you and they will soon be best friends. They buzz around in lazy arcs, occasionally caressing your cheek or touching your hand. There are three ways to deal with their unwanted affections. You can wait until dark and open the windows. You can suck them up in midflight with the hose of your Electrolux (skill required). Or you can install traditional wooden door beads from Provence, which is what we finally did. Apparently, the flies believe the beads form an impenetrable wall, although it's hard to know what flies really believe.

5. Field mice. Well, when you live in the middle of fields, what do you expect? Members of genus *Apodemus* can make themselves scarce for years, then suddenly see you as the Pied Piper. They'll follow you into the house, get into your kitchen drawers, and sometimes even your cotton drawers. One night Sara woke to discover half a dozen furry mice playing hide and seek under the covers. While she thought the mice charming, her friend did not. The remedy for mice is an ultrasonic mouse repeller from Bricomarché. You plug it in and the mice run out—presumably covering their ears.

6. European house spiders. All over Europe? Really? It's a wonder Europeans haven't run screaming all the way to China. These things aren't just spiders. They're *giant mutant tarantulas*. They measure a full meter across—at least in your imagination. Maybe this is caused by their stark appearance, all black and hairy and legs out to there, against the clean white surface of your toilet bowl. Fortunately, any real danger is purely aesthetic. It's been my experience that your wife will happily relocate these beneficial arthropods to the garden where they can scare the bejeesus out of other bugs.

7. Toads. Luckily for you men, your wife gets up at the

crack of dawn to scoop the toads out of the pool. During toad season, she'll discover that one or more members of the species *Bufo bufo* have jumped over the lavender and into the water, with no idea of how to get out. They can swim for a few hours, but hey—Esther Williams they ain't. Throw them a life buoy and get them onto dry land where they can be reunited with their loved ones.

Eileen has a new plan that calls for floating a small square of plywood in the pool with a rope attached. She fully expects to find two dozen toads huddled together like the shivering sailors in Géricault's *Raft of the Medusa,* whereupon she can haul them back to shore. This concept has yet to be tested.

Lesson 14

A Day at the Caves

SARA HAD RECENTLY perfected the art of "French laps." This is a routine in which the athlete paddles up and down the length of the pool in an inflatable easy chair, a glass of pastis in the cupholder. With the days getting hotter, we were thirsty for more water sports. The pool, however, had turned strangely cloudy.

"*Papa?*" said Sara.

"*Oui, ma fille?*"

"Can we go canoeing instead?"

I resisted the urge to say, *Are you nuts? I'm way too old for an extreme sport like canoeing!* The truth is, I wasn't too old, just slightly nervous about climbing into a plastic death trap and shoving it out to the middle of the Dordogne. I looked to Eileen for help.

"It sounds like fun, sweetie, as long as you and Sara do the paddling."

"*Papa,*" said Sara, encouraged, "you've always wanted to see the Lascaux caves. This is the perfect time. We can visit the caves, go canoeing at La Roque-Gageac, and have dinner at

La Belle Étoile."

If Sara could talk me into buying a house, a canoe trip was a piece of *gâteau*. She gave me that look that said she was ten years old again, and I surrendered.

The next morning was glorious and warm. We packed the rented Renault and headed east along the Dordogne River toward Sarlat-la-Canéda. This thriving town is Cave Central for visitors to France. It sits right in the middle of six major sites.

To the west of Sarlat is Font-de-Gaume, the last viewable cave with polychrome paintings. A little further west is the etching-filled Bara-Bahau, named for the sound that huge slabs of rock might have made when they fell from the ceiling thousands of years ago. To the northeast is Rouffignac, where visitors ride a small electric train along a half-mile corridor lined with paintings and etchings. To the north is Lascaux II, a faithful reproduction of the famous original. East of Sarlat is Padirac, technically not a cave but a *gouffre*, a deep abyss. Padirac doesn't have art, but its stalactites and stalagmites give it the majestic look of a prehistoric cathedral. Further away to the southwest lies Pech Merle, with its paintings of spotted horses and its silhouettes of human hands. If you walked up and placed your hand over one of these silhouettes, you would find that even after 25,000 years your hand would perfectly match the size of a Cro-Magnon hand.

Today we were bound for Lascaux. As we drove, the landscape changed from rolling hills and vineyards to forests and rocky outcrops. Golden cliffs curved out over the road, undercut by the carving action of long-ago rivers. Near the tops of the cliffs we could see naturally occurring caves, some of which had been enlarged by human tribes.

I steered the car into the little town of Montignac, down to the Lascaux tourist office. We bought three tickets for the next English-speaking tour, and drove the few remaining miles to the cave.

Our tour group was about twenty people, mostly Dutch and British, along with we three Americans. The group stood in rapt attention as our guide set up the story.

"It was late in the summer of 1940. Marcel Ravidat, a local teenager, was walking with his dog through the woods, looking for buried treasure. Marcel turned and realized his dog was nowhere in sight. He searched frantically in every direction. Finally, he heard a muffled sound over by an old tree. There, stuck in a hole between its gnarled roots, was his frightened dog. He reach down and pulled him out."

A small girl in a print dress muffled a gasp.

"The next day he returned to the hole with three of his friends, bringing a rope and a flashlight. They lowered the skinniest of the four into the hole. Down and down he went. As he touched bottom he switched on the light.

"There it was. The buried treasure. Not a cache of gold and silver, but a magnificent gallery of 16,000-year-old prehistoric paintings. When Picasso saw these, he just shook his head and said, '*Nous n'avons rien inventé.*' We have invented nothing."

Our guide went on to describe the materials the painters

used to make these masterpieces. He pointed out the stumps of candles they brought for illumination, which historians later used to carbon-date the art. With a few waves of his flashlight, he showed how the animals appeared to thunder across the walls of the cave, the way they must have looked in the flickering light of the Cro-Magnons' candles. He then led us through the remaining chambers, explaining the techniques, the tools, and possible meanings of the art.

At the end of the 50-minute tour, we were stunned into silence by the brilliance of our ancestors.

Our guide glanced left and right. "Any questions?"

A few seconds passed. Finally, the small girl in the print dress raised her hand.

"Oui, mademoiselle?"

The child, prodded by her parents, spoke with a trembling British accent.

"Whatever happened to the dog?"

Two bright orange canoes slipped quietly into the shallow green waters of the Dordogne River. Sara took one canoe while Eileen and I shared the other. Sunlight tap-danced on the water ahead. To the right the cliffs of La Roque-Gageac rose like a giant stone curtain. The current carried us effortlessly west toward Bordeaux. A sapphire dragonfly settled on Eileen's hat, contrasting with the golden weave of the straw.

Sara had pulled ahead, and was now gazing up at the

brooding fortress of Castelnaud, high in the hills on our left. Further up on the right another fortress came into view—Beynac, with its fairytale village tumbling down the cliffs to the river. During the Hundred Years' War, Castelnaud was controlled by the English, while the French manned the battlements at Beynac.

What about these place names? Beynac, Lanzac, Bezenac, and Cazenac. Tursac, Plazac, Vézac, and Lupiac. Gignac, Payrignac, Verignac, and Groléjac. Why did so many towns in southwest France end in *ac*? We learned later that *acum* was a Celtic suffix that originally meant *sanctuary*. In the third century *ac* was added to the names of French landowners, whose chateaus would have been the safest places for travelers to rest.

With the light glancing low off the water, we decided two hours of paddling was probably enough for one day. We were hungry, and our sunburned limbs needed relief. We beached our canoes at Beynac, caught the shuttle back to La Roque-Gageac, and washed our feet in a cold outdoor shower. Slipping on our shoes, we walked along the river road to one of the best restaurants on the Dordogne, La Belle Étoile.

There are three great pleasures in life. Eating when you're hungry. Falling asleep when you're tired. And finding love when you're lonely. We were about to partake of the first—made infinitely more pleasurable by the skill of a talented chef.

We sat on the second-floor terrace, an outdoor room bracketed by stone walls and shaded by a vine-covered trellis. In floated the distant squeals of children playing down on the riverbank, squeezing every last second of joy from the day.

The waiter handed out satin-covered menus with gold tassels.

"I keep thinking about those paintings," I said. "All those beautiful animals, layered one over the other. Flowing across the walls, the ceilings, in constant motion. What was the point of all that?"

Sara looked up from her menu. "Maybe they used the cave for religious rituals. Or maybe they had to get psyched up for hunting. The flickering torches made the animals run, like a prehistoric movie. Maybe they sat around beating drums to make the sound of stampeding herds. The drums would echo off the walls like thundering hooves."

"Well," said Eileen, "imagine what it was like in the Vézère Valley 16,000 years ago."

We leaned forward.

"You're a small, weak, naked animal that looks like an hors d'eouvre to a lion or a wolf. You live in a cave because it's safe, a sanctuary high on a cliff. Down below are huge herds—bison, reindeer, aurochs, woolly mammoths—flowing through the valley like a vast river. You can't run as fast as a reindeer, and you couldn't kill one by yourself even if you caught it. Your only real advantage is your brain. And your hands. What do you do with them?"

"You make tools," I said.

"You make tools and weapons, and then you make a plan. You go down to the valley with your friends and surround a stray reindeer. You attack it with spears, then drag the carcass someplace where you can butcher it with stone knives. You carry the pieces back up the cliff, where you can eat the meat in safety for days, maybe weeks."

"Avez-vous choisi?" said the waiter.

"Boy, am I hungry now," said Sara, her eyes comic-book wide.

The waiter went around the table, taking our orders.

"Okay," I said. "Hunting explains the weapons. But what about the art? Why raise your artistic sensibilities to the level of extreme beauty if the main goal is to knock off a few reindeer? Why not just draw some crude diagrams on the wall?

Eileen rolled her eyes. "Because they were *human.* Think about it. Hunting is *how* we live, but beauty is *why* we live. Would you want to go through life without art, or music, or movies, or stories?"

"Kill me now," I said.

The waiter came with our starters. House-made fois gras with roasted figs and raisin toast for Eileen, eggs cocotte with langoustines and morel-infused cream for Sara, a charlotte of white asparagus and fresh goat cheese for me.

"This food," said Eileen. "This is pretty fancy stuff. If the whole idea were only to keep your body alive, why bother making the taste of your food transcendent? If you could just get all your nutrients in a little gray pill, would you skip this meal and take the pill?"

"No way," said Sara, pointing at the ramekin in front of

93

her. "You should try this." We each had a bite. Pure heaven.

"Tell me," said Eileen. "How did you feel when you stood in front of those paintings—even knowing they were reproductions?"

I thought back to the morning. "I felt a sudden shock of recognition. I was standing face to face with my ancestors. Face to face and mind to mind. Time was suddenly collapsed, as if 16,000 years were crushed down to nothing. It was thrilling."

"Exactly. You can read about prehistoric paintings, and look at pictures, but being in their presence—even their fake presence—is transformative. Your world telescopes both ways. You understand you're part of a continuum."

I stood up. "A toast." We raised our glasses of blancs de blancs. "To food, beauty, and the transformative nature of France."

The waiter swept our plates away and replaced them with the next course. Roasted cod with fresh pea and coconut-cream foam. Maigret de canard topped with a seared slab of foie gras. Pistachio-encrusted lamb chops and roasted potato cups filled with chive crème fraîche. Conversation ceased. We ate in silence, thinking about how much we accomplished and how much we learned. It almost didn't matter that we had to leave France in three days. When our dessert of baba au rhum arrived, we were already full. But that didn't stop us.

Lesson 15

St. Georges and the Pool

THE NEXT MORNING the pool was much worse. The once-clear water was now an opaque shade of gray.

"Ugh," said Eileen. "Look at the color." She took the pole net and scooped up an unhappy toad. "We need to do something about this. Fast."

With only two days left before returning to the States, I turned to Peter.

"We should talk to Georges," he said.

"Georges?"

"The French builder who renovated our house. He's forgotten more about pools, plumbing, and local construction methods than most builders will ever know. Christine can give him a ring."

Christine is the translator for the hamlet. She's the only one who can talk to the mayor, the tax office, the electric company, the phone company, the water company—and be understood.

There's a pervasive myth that France has more bureaucracy than other countries. It doesn't. It has *quirkier* bureaucracy. In the United States, when you fill out a form, it stays filled out. It gets processed in a predictable amount of time. The office hours are regular. The people in the offices give you the same information. They behave like public servants. I wouldn't say American bureaucracy is easy, but it's consistent.

In France, you can fill out a change-of-address form and a year later you'll get a letter informing you of a penalty for non-payment. The bill had gone to the old address, even though several bills before it had gone to the new address. Looking closely, you'll notice that the office had waited three months before deciding to charge a penalty. Or one month. Or five months. This is what I mean. Quirky.

Often the only way to resolve a problem is to visit the office in question. I always bring Christine. She not only speaks French, she can usually get the agent to smile.

On one excursion to the tax office we were forced to stand in a long line. When it was finally our turn, the agent pointed his pencil upward and said, *"Premier étage."*

Upon arrival at the office upstairs, the second agent shook his head. *"En bas,"* he said, pointing downstairs.

This time there was no line. The first agent looked up from his desk and said, *"Asseyez-vous,"* gesturing to a row of empty chairs. Before we could even sit down, he said, sharply, *"Approchez!"*

Christine shot back: *"Merci, monsieur. Je peux annuler mon abonnement à la gym"*—I can cancel my gym membership! Down came the officious facade and up went the sides of his mouth. We quickly got what we came for.

I wondered what it would be like to talk with Georges. He certainly wouldn't be a bureaucrat, but my French would be inadequate to discuss the finer points of pools. I prepared a cheat sheet. *Piscine, eau sale, remède, procédé, devis, laps de temps.* Pool, dirty water, remedy, process, cost estimate, time frame. But I would also need Christine's translation skills.

Eileen and Sara had left for the airport. I met Georges and the Johnsons at the front gate, and walked them back to the pool. Georges was a distinguished-looking man of roughly sixty. He had intelligent eyes and a pair of hands that showed he was no stranger to work. He stood at the edge of the pool looking down.

"Oh la la," he said. *"Ce n'est pas bien ça."*

"He says it's not good," Christine translated. "What happened?" she asked. *"Qu'est-ce qui c'est passé?"*

"Il y a de la peinture qui se décolle du fond."

"He says the paint is flaking off the bottom."

Oh no, I thought. *"Quel est le remède?"* I said, glancing at my cheat sheet.

"Vider la piscine," said Georges. *"Et repeindre avec une meilleure peinture."*

"He says drain the pool and start over. They used the wrong kind of paint."

Another setback. I needed a drink. We went into the kitchen.

"Espresso, anyone?" I said. One of the items that came

with the house was an old Nespresso machine. These days you see them everywhere, but at the time it was a revelation. As I passed tiny cups of ristretto to Christine and Peter, I saw Georges down on his haunches, examining the kitchen floor. *"Ces tuiles,"* he said. *"C'est un problème."* He pulled up an old clay tile to reveal a mass of roots growing from a dirt foundation. We looked on in horror.

"The floor is dirt?" I said. "That must be why the tiles rock when you walk on them. They're not glued down!"

"It's pretty common in old farmhouses," said Peter. "Everything's built on dirt."

Georges pointed to the old wisteria outside the kitchen window, then down to the floor. *"Les racines vont sous le plancher."*

"He says the roots are running under the floor and pushing up the tiles."

I was dreading Eileen's return. We would need something stronger than espresso.

"Georges," I said, making a writing motion with my hand, *"un devis pour le plancher aussi?"* I asked for an estimate on the kitchen floor as well as the pool. I knew Dennis would have disapproved of removing the 400-year-old tiles, but the floor was getting worse. The roots would soon be growing up through the cracks.

"Je vais enlever le sol et le remplacer par du béton."

"He says he can dig out the floor and pour concrete. Then cover it with new handmade tiles."

Georges paced the kitchen floor both ways and wrote some numbers in a small notebook. He went outside and paced off the pool. He wrote out a *devis* to take back with us. Some souvenir. I thanked Christine and Peter, and told Georges I'd be in touch.

When Eileen got back I told her about the pool and the floor. She sat down.

"We don't have much choice," she said glumly. "I didn't tell you before," she said, "but I've always hated that floor. It's unsanitary and uncleanable. It gives me the creeps. But now the pool, too."

We would later come to view Georges as a friend and a savior, but at the moment all we a saw was a setback. We had a drink, then started to pack for the long flight home. Our "restored" farmhouse was looking more and more like a mirage.

Lesson 16

The Bodega Beckons

TEN MONTHS LATER, our plane landed with a bump on the Bergerac-Roumanières tarmac. I woke from a jetlagged sleep. Eileen was looking out the window toward the south, where a curl of smoke was rising from a nearby vineyard. We were exhausted but excited. The summer was just starting.

Our footsteps crunched on the gravel as we trudged through the courtyard to the back of the house. The lavenders lining the pool were alive with violet flowers and frantically buzzing bees. The pool was crystal clear with a new pale-blue paint job.

Back around at the front door, I reached into my pocket for the keys. We entered the kitchen and breathed the familiar scent of fuel oil and sisal. The new floor was gorgeous. Irregular handmade tiles, laid perfectly flat from wall to wall, with the lower cabinets reinstalled and the heavy Godin stove repositioned. Georges had done a fine job.

On the counter were a box of cookies and a fresh baguette, and in the fridge, containers of butter, cheese, and milk. There was a vase of purple flowers on the table with a note from Christine: "Welcome home, Americans. Come over when you get settled. Dinner is on."

The Johnsons moved to France fifteen years ago on the orders of a doctor. Peter's health had been suffering from the increasing stress of his engineering job, so his physician issued one of the best prescriptions ever written: "Go to France and drink red wine," he said. "Your working days are over."

Since then the two Brits have woven themselves into the fabric of the community—Christine with her unfailing friendliness and serviceable French, and Peter with his computer savvy and ability to fix anything. Most of their friends are French, even though Peter doesn't speak a word of the language. He simply converses in English, and his friends converse in French. It's not clear how they understand each other, but they do.

"Oy! Come in, you two, come in," said Peter as we ascended the steps of the veranda. Pots of flowers and herbs lined the way. Black cats scattered as we entered the kitchen.

"It won't be much," said Christine, waving toward the stove. "Just some odds and sods I've thrown together." Christine can cook anything. If you gave her an old shoe it would come back as boeuf bourguignon. She grows her own vegetables and fruits, cooking and storing many of these over the winter. In the summer her garden is ablaze with flowers. *Belles de nuit* of every color spill over the beds, and English roses climb vigorously up the side of the barn. Her only gardening failure is tomatoes; they don't seem to like the off-and-on weather of France.

"The Bodega is this Sunday," said Peter, shutting his laptop. "You're cutting it close, Yanks."

The Bodega is our annual community party. It takes over the medieval village of Issigeac at the beginning of July. The air is filled with the music of marching bands, rock groups, and drum circles from the surrounding villages, all competing for the attention of tourists and locals. Food stalls and wine stands line the square. After a few glasses of vin rouge, people are likely to dance at the drop of a hat.

"Wow, I thought it was next week," I said.

"They moved it up." Peter suffers through the cold winters and rainy springs with a single thought in mind: the Bodega is coming. If we miss it, he's heartbroken. He and Christine only stay for an hour or two, but that hour or two makes all the difference. Summer in the Dordogne begins with the Issigeac Bodega.

Sunday night. Crowds pour into the village—French and British and Dutch and German. We say hello to a few Americans who are passing through on an extended tour of Europe. Sara has flown in from New York and is now scooping up plastic cups of Bergerac rosé from the Domaine du Siorac stand. She hands them out two by two as a young volunteer places them on the plywood counter.

In France, when hundreds of people get together and drink

wine, there are never fights, just fun. In America, we have no such expectation. If a public event features the sale of alcohol, it's almost guaranteed that we'll need gun-toting security guards or uniformed police to keep us in line. Here in France the police are a rare sight. People simply behave. This allows the wine to play its intended role as a natural accompaniment to food and social lubricant.

Interestingly, when normally rowdy tourists visit France, they too start to behave. It's as if they come to France to *find* their inhibitions. We like to think when they go home and unpack their suitcases there's a little *savoir-faire* lying among the souvenirs.

One of the greatest charms of the Bodega—or one of its irritations, depending on your view—is that a wide range of pop, rock, drum, and marching bands all play their music at the same time, often only twenty yards apart. Your musical education isn't complete until you've heard John Philip Sousa blending with Bossa Nova, Dire Straits colliding head on with *La Vie en Rose*. There's little chance of getting a song stuck in your head unless it comes tangled with two or three others.

The five of us flow with the crowd through the narrow, winding streets, hoping to catch a glimpse of our favorite marching band, the Bluettes. Not unlike the other drum and tuba groups, the Bluettes are a mixture of male and female, young and old, novice and expert. But there's something special about this one, an *esprit de corps* we find disarming. We've watched the younger musicians grow up year after year, as if viewed in a series of snapshots, a stop-motion animation of aging. The blue and white uniforms never change, but the faces elongate, shift, widen. The girls braid their hair, cut it short, grow it long, dye it purple, and get it styled. The boys start as cherubs, morph into imps, outgrow their pants, deepen their voices, sprout ghostly beards, and hang out with girls. For us, this has been one of the payoffs of planting ourselves here—a feeling of continuity, of seeing French life as a movie instead of a postcard.

Issigeac is not a bastide but an older medieval village. Built in a circle instead of a grid, its streets curve and weave in a bewildering spiral pattern. Tourists quickly lose their direction and end up walking in circles, necks craned to take in the handsome herringbone walls and weathered wood shutters of the half-timbered houses.

To make navigation more baffling, the village is transformed in different ways by different events. The springtime brings the Marché aux Fleurs, a garden show that paints the streets with brightly colored flowers, filling your eyes and flooding your nostrils. In the summer, the outdoor market explodes every Sunday morning, scattering stalls of food, clothing, baskets, and jewelry throughout the town. In July, the Foire aux Paniers brings in thousands of tourists to buy beautiful willow baskets and woven ornaments, including the Bouyricou-style baskets that echo the spiral pattern of the streets. Later in July, the summer brocante decorates the village with antique furniture and bric-a-brac, and in August the village is alive with jugglers and actors dressed in medieval costumes.

The locals here have it made. They can choose from three bakeries, two grocery stores, three bars, two pharmacies, and four restaurants. There's a butcher shop, a tobacco shop, a bank, and a post office, along with several antique shops and art galleries.

Peter knows every house for sale in Issigeac. He also knows every cat that has ever graced a gatepost. His dream is to move into one of these houses, where Christine can grow pink roses up the stone wall and their cats can stand sentinel on their very own gateposts.

"This one would make a great little house," he says, stopping in front of two-story stone building. There's a garage door below and two windows above it, each with a decorative carved-stone casement. "That garage could be the perfect salon. Can you imagine a big, beautiful French window where the door is?" An orange-and-white cat rubs against his pant leg.

"Absolutely," says Sara, her eyes working in x-ray mode. "With a nice little kitchen at the back."

Continuing down the crooked street, we round the corner at the back of the old church.

"Les Touristes!" cries Eileen. Four musicians wearing white pants, Hawaiian shirts, and pork-pie hats pounded out a version of *Mrs. Robinson* that was vaguely recognizable as the Simon and Garfunkel song. The band's specialty is "musical tourism," a pastiche of styles and songs from the worldwide pop canon. Two little girls of seven or eight, all dimples and missing teeth, perform a synchronized go-go routine out in front while a glamorous mother looks on, cigarette held between long fingers. Off to the side, couples begin dancing the Lindy Hop with wine-tinged abandon.

The hours roll by and the Johnsons head home, leaving the three of us to wander the village by ourselves. The sky slowly turns purple, contrasting with the yellow bulbs that glow from strings over the street. A boy leans out of an upper-story window while his grandmother looks up from an open doorway below. Knots of teenagers jostle with parents and their kids, moving like schools of fish through the darkening lanes. Up ahead is a rockabilly band singing an Elvis song in a thick French accent. It sounds a little like English, but the words aren't quite right.

> *Since my baby lifts me,*
> *I find a new place do twell—*
> *A town at the end of lonely street-a, Artbreak Otel.*
> *You maybe so lonely, babe-a, I give so lonely…*

I turn and shout to Sara, "That takes me back." When I look around she's gone. Eileen points over my shoulder. Sara is down the *lonely street-a*, pulling some money from her purse. She comes back with a large plate of braised ham and duck-fat potatoes.

"Hungry?" she says. We sit on a window ledge and eat our

dinner while a drum group swivels and sways in the square in front of us.

When we get back to the house around midnight, our ears are still ringing. We can't get the mashup of *Artbreak Otel* and *Colonel Bogey March* out of our heads.

Leave It to Cleaver

EVERY WEDNESDAY and Saturday the Bergerac organic market, or *marché bio,* encircles the Église Notre-Dame. The church's elegant spire is the pin that fixes the city to the map. Bergerac is full of contrasts. On the one hand it's a tourist destination with a fascinating mix of architecture, and on the other it's a workaday town with peeling plaster and a crumbling infrastructure. The view you get depends on the weather. On a cloudy day the town seems dingy and depressing. On a bright day it looks charming and cheerful.

Today the sun poured freely into the city center, painting the buildings with gold highlights and cobalt shadows. Scores of colorful food stalls spiraled out from the church to the main parking lot, spreading onto the sidewalk that borders the ancient lanes of the *vieille ville,* the old town.

Parking on market days is *très difficile.* Your best bet is to drive around to the north end of town and squeeze between a Renault Clio and a Fiat 500, often parking halfway over the curb. While the police are lenient on market days, the residents are not. You must never—*jamais!*—block someone's garage access or impede a motorist's progress. The offended party will have your car hooked up to a tow truck before you can say *bonjour*. Locals are acutely aware of these rules, even as they park in the oddest of spots.

Sara and I left the car on the curved corner of an intersection—normally a *non-non*—and walked south to the bio. The sky was a deep and cloudless blue on the Wednesday after the Bodega. We carried shopping bags and wore straw hats against the intense rays of the July sun.

"What are we looking for?" I asked Sara.

"Something for tonight. I was thinking a turkey roulade with grilled courgettes, along with those yummy duck-fat potatoes we had at the Bodega. We can use up the duck fat we already have in the fridge." She stopped at a crowded stall and bought a kilo of fingerling potatoes.

The market stalls in this part of France are a feast for the eyes. Bins of bright red radishes contrast with pure white leeks laid side by side with their curly white roots entwining. Cartons of stubby orange carrots lie beside luscious bunches of deep green parsley. Endive bulbs live next door to bonbon tomatoes, and boxes of haricots verts cozy up to crates of fresh green mâche. Charming handwritten signs, displaying the names and prices, wave insouciantly from various boxes.

I looked up and found Sara standing in front of a butcher's truck, examining a skinless creature that hung upside down from the top of the window.

"What is it?" I asked.

"*Lapin.* A rabbit. What if I made a delicious fricassée instead of the turkey roulade? Rabbit is such a classic."

I hid my horror. A whole rabbit? Really? With the head still on it? I tried to dissuade her. "Isn't rabbit stew a winter dish? You know, for the long cold nights in December? It's so hot right now."

"Naw, it'll be cooler by tonight. Let's go for it." She pulled a wad of euros from her purse. The butcher rolled the rabbit in paper and placed it in a bag. While I love to watch Sara cook, I wasn't sure this was an operation I wanted to observe.

The sun had arced around to the far side of the house. The light from the shaded courtyard came through the windows to give the kitchen a cold cast. Sara stood with a chef's knife in her hand. A skinny pink body lay on the cutting board, positioned horizontally under the halogen track lamps. She placed the blade of the knife against the rabbit's neck. Using the heel of her hand she shoved down hard. Crunch. The blade cut deeply, but the head stayed on.

I was standing back against the kitchen door with my hands over my face. I peeked through my fingers. "Did it come off?"

She felt around the rabbit's neck and peered into the gash made by the knife. "I'm not sure I found the space between the vertebrae." She repositioned the knife and got ready shove it downwards. Her hands were shaking.

"Everything okay?" I said, squinting through my fingers.

She stood staring at the rabbit, both hands on the knife. "I can't do it. I can't. It looks too much like a cat." She looked at me imploringly, her lips mouthing a silent *s'il te plaît.*

"Oh, jeez. You want *me* to cut the head off a cat? Can't we just bring it back and have the butcher do it?"

"M-O-M!" she yelled, quickly casting me as the weak, ineffective parent, which in this case was accurate. "Mom, the head won't come off!"

Eileen came in from the salon. She looked at Sara, then at me, then at the rabbit. She took the knife from Sara and set it on the countertop. "Step aside," she said, pulling a heavy cleaver from the knife rack.

Sara and I backed slowly towards the bedroom door. Eileen raised the cleaver, using both arms for maximum force. Sara slipped around the corner and pulled me into the bedroom. We closed the door and waited for axe to fall.

Silence.

We opened the door a crack. Eileen stood there, arms raised, tears streaming down her face.

"What's wrong, Mom?" said Sara.

"I can't."

Sara looked at me.

"I used to have a little Dutch bunny," said Eileen. "His name was Wabbit."

"Rabbit?" said Sara.

"Not Rabbit. *Wabbit.* You know, 'You cwazy wabbit'?" She

lowered the cleaver. "I just can't."

Sara and I ventured cautiously back into the kitchen. Eileen suddenly jerked back, let loose a tortured yell, and down came the guillotine. WHACK! —the head shot off the table, bounced against the lower cabinets, and rolled to a stop at our feet. On its face was a strangely serene expression, as if nothing at all had happened. Eileen was sobbing. She pushed past us, ran into the bedroom, and slammed the door.

I turned to Sara. "It's okay, sweetie. Start cooking. She'll be all right."

I followed Eileen into the bedroom, sat next to her, and put my hand on her shoulder. She lay face down with a pillow over her head, shuddering from the mental image of a decapitated childhood pet.

Her voice was muffled. "Wabbit."

I went back into the kitchen and poured two glasses of rosé. I paused, and poured a third. "Here," I said to Sara, and headed back to the bedroom.

Two hours later, out on the terrace, the table was set, the candles lit. Eileen's eyes were still swollen and red. I uncorked a bottle of pinot noir. Sara brought out dishes of fingerling potatoes and carrots, both roasted in duck fat. Duck fat is considered by some to be a "healthy fat" because it lowers your unhealthy cholesterol. Others disagree. Who cares? You'll never taste anything better.

"Sorry, Mom," said Sara. "I shouldn't have asked you to do that." She brought out three dishes plated with lapin à la moutarde, rabbit with mustard sauce, and placed them on the table.

"No one ever said being French would be easy," I said, pouring the pinot. Eileen and Sara nodded as if I'd just said something profound.

Eileen stood up. "Here's to dear, departed Wabbit." We clinked our glasses. "Rest in peace, old friend."

The three of us ate our meal by candlelight, serenaded by a lone cicada. The gentle breezes of a warm July evening mixed the scent of lavender with the aromas of the roasted vegetables and rabbit fricasée. The creamy mustard sauce went perfectly with the fresh fingerlings.

We talked about the differences between French and American cuisine. We expressed our gratitude for the embarrassment of riches found at the outdoor markets—the juicy ripe fruits, the bountiful vegetables, the interesting meats and cheeses.

And then we talked of *pétanque*. This was a game we would need to learn if we hoped to become part of the village. An informal tournament was only two days away.

LAPIN À LA MOUTARDE
Rabbit with Mustard

Lesson learned: Have your butcher cut the rabbit up for you, or at least remove the head! Brown the rabbit well in the skillet—it ensures that your stew will have a deep, complex flavor.
—*Sara*

    1 three-pound rabbit, cut into 12 pieces
    1/3 cup Dijon mustard
    2 tablespoons vegetable or olive oil
    4 ounces lardons fumés
        (or 4 slices thick-cut smoked bacon, diced)
    18 white pearl onions, peeled
    2 teaspoons fresh thyme leaves, roughly chopped
    1/2 teaspoon chopped fresh rosemary
    1 bay leaf
    Salt and freshly ground pepper to taste
    2 cups dry white wine (we use Bergerac sec)
    1/3 cup crème fraîche

1. Place rabbit in a medium bowl and toss with mustard until it is thoroughly coated. Cover and refrigerate at least two hours or overnight.

2. When ready to cook, heat oil in a large high-sided skillet over medium high heat. Add lardons and cook until golden and crispy; remove with a slotted spoon and reserve for later. Add onions to skillet and cook until golden, stirring occasionally, about 8 minutes. Transfer onions to a small bowl using a slotted spoon, and add rabbit pieces to skillet. Cook rabbit until nicely browned, 5–8 minutes per side.

3. Add thyme, rosemary, bay leaf, salt, pepper, reserved onions, and wine. Bring to a boil, cover, and cook at a low simmer until rabbit is tender, about 40 minutes. Stir in crème fraîche, and adjust seasoning with more salt and pepper if necessary. Serve over roasted vegetables, mashed potatoes, or pasta. Sprinkle reserved crispy lardons over top.

Serves 6

☞ Photos and printable versions are at **www.beginningfrench.com**

Lesson 18

The Rules of Boules

ANTON CROUCHES, motionless. He cups a scuffed metal ball in his right hand, his face the picture of concentration. Seconds go by. A minute. The other players are silent as they wait for his throw. Then, without moving the rest of his body so much as a centimeter, he turns his hand over and flips the ball into the air. It floats there as if the law of gravity has been suspended. When the ball comes down with a thud, it rolls to within inches of the marker.

Robert shakes his head. *"Boule devant, boule d'argent."* A front ball is a money ball. It can easily block opponents from getting closer to the marker.

Friday night is boules night in the village. The official name of *boules* is *pétanque,* meaning "feet fixed." There's no difference between pétanque and boules, but boules is one syllable shorter, so in our book it wins. The boules court is a flat, sandy patch in back of the village *salle des fêtes,* the town's banquet hall. Mature trees surround the court, and floodlights hang from the trees to illuminate late games.

Anyone can show up and get on a team. Regulars are Anton

and Sophie, Robert and Jeannine, Jean-Pierre and Josette, and Peter and Christine. The four couples are usually joined by Gilbert, Marco, and Baako, older men who live nearby. Then there's Aimée, a sassy teenager who arrives by motorcycle and cries *"Oh, putain!"* whenever she misses a shot. But the de facto leader of the group is Jean-Pierre. We're not exactly sure why this is. He's short and shy with a round belly held in place by a sleeveless undershirt. Not the classic attributes of a leader—but leader he is.

The objective of the game is simple: To get your boules closer to the marker ball, or *cochonnet,* than those of your opponent. (*Cochonnet* is French for "piglet," named for its smaller size; some are even pink.) There are two sets of rules for achieving the objective: the official rules and the village rules.

For example, the official rules call for no more than three players per team. In the village, it's come one, come all. If people show up late, Jean-Pierre just sticks them on a team and gives the other team a couple of extra throws.

In the official rules, players are required to toss their boules from within a perfect circle drawn exactly 50 centimeters in diameter. In the village, players throw from behind a scuff mark made by Josette with the heel of her shoe.

The official rules say that each player's boules must have a pattern of lines that distinguishes them from those of the other players. In the village, players tell their boules apart by the number of scratches and the color of the rust.

I was delighted when Sara gave me a set of boules for my

birthday. Yet whenever I use them I feel slightly embarrassed. The best players have boules that are dark and rough with age; mine are still as shiny as silver dollars. When everyone's boules are thrown, mine stand out from the others, usually somewhere outside the grouping. I feel this is a metaphor.

Josette steps up to the line with a boule in each hand. She's the polar opposite of Anton. Anton plays like a professional—muscular, precise, strategic. Josette just walks up to the line with a giggle and tosses the ball. If the throw happens to be a crucial one, she'll stick out her tongue for added accuracy. Surprisingly, Anton's and Josette's styles seem to be equally effective.

Josette's first ball lands just to the side of Anton's. *"Merde, pas là!"* She throws her arms up in disbelief. Her second ball is right on target. It nudges Anton's slightly to the left, replacing it with her own and holding the point for the team. She does a little victory dance, chubby arms and legs flying every which way.

"Pas mal," says Anton, grudgingly.

Next up is Baako. Baako and Marco originally came from Italy, so they speak a sort of "Fritalian."

"Troppo fort!" says Marco, as he throws his boule too hard, sending it past the cochonnet. He mutters something decidedly un-French, and casts his eyes heavenward. Taking a deep breath, he goes back to the line. His second ball falls short. *"Oh, la la. Maintenant troppo faible!"* Too weak!

Josette says that the ball probably hit a *caillou*—a pebble.

"Ce n'est pas de ta faute," she says, touching his arm. He seems reassured to think the pebble may be at fault.

Peter goes next. He's tall and thin compared to the French, and looks more like cricket bowler than a boules player. He's about to go into shooting mode. Shooting is a strategy in which the player throws the ball hard enough to knock an opponent's boule away from the cochonnet, or the cochonnet away from an opponent's boule.

Just as Peter is about to throw, Robert emits a barely audible clucking noise. Peter stops in mid-windup. He puts his hands on his hips, tilts his head, and stares at Robert. Their running joke is that Peter turns chicken whenever he throws. Robert looks away and feigns innocence.

Peter winds up again, and Robert clucks again. This time Peter follows through and his boule misses Josette's by a mile, skittering off into the trees. Robert can't contain a guffaw.

On his second throw, Peter is ready for him, and he knocks Josette's boule off to the right with an explosive crack, leaving the cochonnet open.

Up comes Marco, a man so old that he doesn't actually walk. He simply rocks back and forth while leaning forward. His throwing style is a miracle of efficiency: he stands ramrod straight under his sailor hat, imagining the course of the boule; then he opens his hand. The boule rolls down his fingers, onto the ground, and continues to the target as if pulled by a magnet.

This time it rolls up to the cochonnet and holds the point.

Jeannine is the last to go. Her throwing style could be described as no style at all. Most players lead with the back of the hand as they lob the boule into the air, but Jeannine just tosses it out there underhand.

Her boule lands short of Marco's, then rolls up close to it. So close, in fact, that all the players rush up to see who has won the round. Jean-Pierre stares at the two balls and the cochonnet. He squints and rubs his chin. He looks at Robert, who is walking from one side to the other to get a better view. Sophie says it's Jeannine. Christine thinks it's Marco. Members of both teams are down on their haunches to get a better look at the situation. Opinions are running about fifty-fifty. There's no resolution in sight.

"Attention!" I shout. I'm standing just outside the group, waving my iPhone. On the screen is the Pétanque-ometer, a clever little app that David Stuart told me about. You hold your phone over the cochonnet, and the app draws concentric rings to show precisely which ball is closest. I push my way into the middle of the group. *"Regardez,"* I say, lining up the phone with the boules. The whole group leans in. They look at the phone. They look at me.

Then Robert starts clucking. Low at first, then louder. Soon everyone is imitating a chicken. "Look at the screen," I say, "It's Jeannine. Jeannine is closest!" The clucking gives way to out-and-out heckling.

"Merci, monsieur iPhone," says Robert. He turns to the crowd: *"Mesdames et messieurs, c'est Steve Jobs!"*

Aimée runs over to a lavender bush and breaks off a length of stem. She runs back and stretches it from the cochonnet to one boule, and then to the other. She looks up at Jean-Pierre.

"*C'est Marco!*" he cries. The players nod their heads in agreement. Jean-Pierre looks at me pityingly, and says I can throw out the marker to start the next round.

"*Allez, monsieur iPhone,*" he says, handing me the cochonnet. Eileen and Sara beam from the sidelines. We were in.

A Little Night Music

THE KITCHEN WENT DARK. Again. Sara opened the door to let in the last of the daylight.

The electricity at Le Rêve was never robust. Whenever we turned on the dishwasher and the toaster, it went out. Whenever we turned on the dryer and the microwave, it went out. Whenever we turned on the washer, the dryer, and the Nespresso machine, it went out. It reached the point where we feared to turn on the radio.

Usually the remedy was simple: go to the wooden box on the wall of the salon and push the black button. There were instructions inside the box, thoughtfully prepared by Dennis Henderson. But this time the black button didn't work. The house stayed dark, and right now Peter wasn't around to help.

"What'll we do about dinner?" said Eileen.

"Why don't we go to the night market?" offered Sara.

"It's Sunday," I said. "All the markets are closed."

"No, no," said Sara. "The *night market*. In Monbazillac. Remember? We saw a sign for *marché nocturne* on the road. You buy your dinner from food trucks and local producers.

Everyone gathers around long picnic tables. It sounds like fun!"

Little Monbazillac is a village that sits on a ridge overlooking the town of Bergerac. The world knows it best for its wine—a sweet golden drink made possible by weather that creates the "noble rot." When fog from the Dordogne Valley settles up against the low-lying hills, it rots the grapes in a way that increases their sweetness. While most of the area's excellent reds and whites are priced around six euros, bottles of Monbazillac can sell for twenty euros or more. As a result, the village is prosperous, progressive, and inordinantly happy. This prosperity dates back to at least the 16th century, as evidenced by the elegant Chateau Monbazillac, now one of the area's most popular tourist attractions.

We pulled into a parking lot in back of the co-op tasting room and walked across to the church. In the adjacent open space, strings of lights hung in crisscrossed garlands from the tops of pine trees. Underneath were scores of picnic tables with white plastic chairs.

The tables were mostly filled by now, but we managed to find one with three empty places at the end. At the other end, four generations of a French family had just settled down for their Sunday dinner.

"Jean-Claude," said the great grandmother, *"tu es un bon garçon."*

The good son, a sixtyish grandfather with the build of a bricklayer, was balancing plates of *moules et frites* as he carried them to the table. He placed a *barquette* of mussels in front of his mother and poured out the wine. He raised a glass to the family.

"La vie est belle," he said, grinning broadly, and gave his elderly mother a kiss on the cheek. She blushed and took a sip. Eileen and I smiled at each other. *This* was why we came to France.

Sara had taken off down the midway in search of food. Meanwhile, Eileen got up to visit a nearby wine stand. She brought back a bottle of rosé and three plastic cups. The night markets give local wine producers a chance to show off their products, so they discount their bottles to around five euros. The same quality of wine in California would cost the equivalent of fifteen or twenty euros.

"Look what *I* found," Sara sang with a taunting melody. She held out two paper plates piled high with spit-roasted pork and sautéed scalloped potatoes. "You should taste this. They stick slivers of garlic under the skin, then roast the pork over a bed of burning grapevines. The gravy has pepper and Monbazillac wine in it."

We devoured the pork and potatoes in blissful silence, too engrossed in the textures and flavors of the food to talk. When we finished the wine, Eileen went over to another booth and bought strawberries and chantilly for dessert. We began to wonder: How could food like this be possible for seven euros a person? No wonder these families show up every Sunday. They could never afford to cook like this at home.

"Look at that French family," Eileen said about our tablemates. "They brought their own dinnerware." The young grandfather had come with a special knife on his belt to open the moules. His wife had brought a panier of dishes, flatware, wine glasses, and cloth napkins to spread out on the table. The three of us looked at our paper plates, plastic cups, plastic forks, and plastic knives with sudden disdain. It was time to become French.

Monbazillac marked the beginning of our love affair with the night markets. We quickly discovered a number of other markets that fall on different days of the week. Monday nights in Beaumont, Tuesday nights in Eymet, Wednesday nights in Belves, Thursday nights in Issigeac, and Friday nights in Sigoules. With a little driving you can eat out every night of the week for less than it costs to cook at home.

The following summer we discovered the night market in Duras. A charming hill town about 40 minutes from Le Rêve, Duras competes for Thursday nights with the Issigeac market. So we save it for special occasions. What makes it worth the longer drive is the size of the crowd, the quality of the food, and the joyfulness of the music. One of the most popular acts in Duras is a one-man band with an array of prerecorded backups, and—wait for it—an accordion.

You may have read the bumper sticker that says, "Use an accordion, go to jail." Or possibly the other one, "Accordions don't kill people, people do." Or maybe you fondly recall the classic: "Friends don't let friends play the accordion." Go ahead and laugh. But there's something about an accordion in a French village that renders such cynicism meaningless. A young man with an accordion jumps up on stage to rally the crowd. People abandon their dinners and dash to the dance floor. As many as a hundred people at a time will be up there doing the waltz, the Lindy, or a line dance.

"We should learn how to do this," said Eileen, swaying to the chorus of *Lady of Spain*.

I looked at her. Normally, I would say something like, "Get a grip. It's the wine. In the morning you'll come back to your senses." But instead I found myself saying, "Yes, we *should* learn how to do this."

When Sara returned from her food-scouting expedition with some good news, Eileen interrupted her report: "We're going to learn how to dance!"

"Really? How cool!"

Sara *would* say that. She, who has spent so many weekends swing-dancing until the wee hours of the morning. The night-clubs of Manhattan and Brooklyn would be far less profitable without the continuing patronage of Sara. But I can't believe *I'd* said it. With any luck, by tomorrow we'll forget this ever happened.

"What about the food?" I said, changing the subject.

"Well, we've got two great choices. There's a man who sells foie gras sautéed in sweet liqueur with peaches, and another man who sells duck burgers."

"Duck burgers?" I said. "Is that just a hamburger with ground duck instead of beef?"

"It's much better than that. It's ground duck with herbs, sandwiched in a baguette with goat cheese and onion jam. Looks yummy."

"Let's get one of each and share," said Eileen.

So we did. We used the foie gras as our entree, along with a small glass of Monbazillac. Then we bought a bottle of Duras rouge to go with the duckburger. Both courses were out of this world. We went back for seconds of each.

The next morning Sara sat down at the kitchen table and wrote out a recipe for duck burgers. She's the kind of chef who can stand in front of the stove, staring into space, and imagine how ingredients might combine to make culinary magic. She emits little smacking sounds as she tests out the various options on her mental taste buds.

That afternoon she ground up some duck and successfully duplicated the experience of the night before. If anything, it was slightly improved by the addition of sautéed shallots in the meat.

Happily, there was no further talk of dancing.

Lesson 20

Shall We Dance?

BACK TO THE PROBLEM of electricity. It's my philosophy that if it ain't broke, don't fix it. Furthermore, if it's starting to break, don't fix it. Finally, if it's actually broke, pour yourself a glass of rosé, saunter out to the terrace, and ask yourself, *Do I really need to fix it?*

When we got back to the house after the Monbazillac night market, the black button in the electrical box decided to work and the electricity popped back on. I don't ask questions.

But now I had a more serious problem. A few weeks after discovering duck burgers in Duras, we were driving through our little village on the way back from Leclerc. Eileen spotted one of those A-frame menu boards that advertise *"Menu du Jour, 19 Euros"* off to the side of the road. Except this one said, "Dance Lessons, Tuesday Night."

I don't know about you, but when I see a sign like that I avert my eyes. I can't think of anything worse than paying good money to publicly demonstrate my lack of grace and coordination. Obviously, Eileen had no such qualms.

"We were just thinking about learning to dance, and here

it is, a sign. Literally!"

My mind raced. "Tuesday," I said. "Isn't that when we go to the Issigeac night market?"

"No, sweetie, that's Thursday. Tuesday is the Eymet night market. They only serve moules and frites. Besides, the sign was in *English!*"

With a single stroke she wiped out my second argument. A sign in English means lessons in English. This instructor had our number. I realized that my next step was going to be a dance step.

"Let's do it," I said, giving the words as much enthusiasm as I could muster. Why compound fear with inconsistency? A few weeks ago I said it was a good idea, so it should be a good idea now. I just needed to locate my inner trooper.

The *salle polyvalente,* or multipurpose room, was filling up fast with nervous students. They came from a variety of backgrounds and age groups. There was an older English couple who brought their own dance shoes; a tall, thin young man, probably French, who tried against the odds to be invisible; two women in their thirties, one large, one small, who seemed to be good friends; three teenage girls we recognized from the beer stall at the Bodega; and a man in his fifties with ill-fitting pants. There were about twenty students in all, including Anton and Sophie from Friday night boules.

A confident young man glided to the center of the floor

and clapped his hands twice. A woman in her forties followed him.

"*Bonsoir à tous,*" he said in a loud, clear voice. "My name is Tony. This is Bérénice. We are your instructors for the Tuesday dance. *Ça va?*"

Everyone responded *ça va.*

"Bérénice teach the advance class, I teach the beginner. Please go with your class you sign up with."

A group of seven people, including Anton and Sophie and the English couple, followed Bérénice to the far side of the dance floor. Our group of thirteen stayed with Tony.

"In this class we do West Coast Swing," said Tony. Eileen and I looked at each other. We're *from* the West Coast. We've never heard of West Coast Swing. Is it the west coast of France, maybe, or the west coast of Australia?

"These are the dance you have all the time in France—at the night club, the wedding, the Bodega in Issigeac, and so on. After you learn the West Coast Swing, we go to try the Lindy Hop and the Charleston."

Eileen whispered, "The Charleston? What is this, 1925?"

"The leader—the man—line up on this side. The lady line up on that side. We have seven man and six lady, so I will be the lady, too."

Tony went over to the music system and put on Wilson Pickett's classic, "In the Midnight Hour." He demonstrated the basic six-count rhythm: "*Un. Deux. Trois et quatre. Cinq et six.*" With each count he shifted his weight from one foot to the other. "Now you try, and count it loud."

"*Un. Deux. Trois et quatre. Cinq et six.*" We repeated the rhythm together, doing our best to mimic his movements. When half the song was done, he stopped the music and showed us how to apply the rhythm to the steps.

At first I did everything wrong. When the dancers stepped backward, I stepped forward. When they turned right, I turned left. When they paused for a beat, I kept going. Eileen seemed to be doing fine.

It dawned on me that learning to dance would be a matter of overcoming my inborn tendency to do everything backwards. My first instinct is almost always opposite of what it should be. When I drive up to an unfamiliar intersection and have to decide which way to go, I'll usually choose the wrong direction and have to make a U-turn. When I emerge from my hotel room in the morning, I'll automatically turn the wrong way and wonder what happened to the elevator. When I have to make a business decision, I'll sometimes pick the counterintuitive path. This is a powerful strategy if your goal is to innovate. But if your goal is to dance, it's just wrong.

By the end of the lesson, Eileen was staying with the rhythm and getting the steps right. Her ability to grasp these concepts was impressive. Sara would be proud. Myself—well, I was able to reverse most of my natural tendencies and get into semi-sync with the rest of the dancers.

"Whew! That was draining," said Eileen. "I need a glass of rosé. *Tout de suite!*"

Tony came over and pulled us aside. "Listen," he said. "I don't know how to say. You two are not beginners."

I was dumbfounded. He must have spotted something special in us—some latent talent that only a true professional could see.

"You are not beginners. You are *pre*-beginners. I think you must take private lessons before you can join this group."

My mouth fell open. Eileen inhaled deeply and raised her eyes to the ceiling. She finally asked, "That bad?"

Tony was apologetic. *"Désolé."*

On Saturday morning we took our first private lesson. All we did was work on rhythm.

Correction: All *I* did was work on rhythm. Eileen watched. Tony was determined to get me up to speed so that I could eventually dance with my pre-beginner partner. In other words, I was *pre-pre*-beginner.

He put on some music and told me to count out the rhythm: *Un. Deux. Trois et quatre. Cinq et six.* No problem—I passed with flying colors. Then he said to move my feet while I counted. The numbers and the moves refused to mesh. It was as if my feet ceased to think. Or maybe they were thinking too much. I tried to stop my feet from thinking. No luck. I looked at Eileen. Her eyes were shut and she was slowly shaking her head.

"Okay," said Tony, "Let's try something new. Just walk to

the music in time. Right, left, right, left, right, left."

Normally, this wouldn't be a problem. I walk all the time. I can even walk and listen to music. But somehow focusing on right and left made it more complicated.

"Just walk!" said Tony, exasperated.

I was walking, but it wasn't a normal, human walk. I looked like R2-D2 with a faulty circuit. We continued this way for an hour, then he stopped the music.

"Okay, okay," he said. "Now I work with Eileen." He took her hand and smoothly pulled her forward as he stepped backward. They went through the basic swing routine without a hitch.

"You can count!" he cried with relief. Then he looked at me. "See? Simple."

Going home in the car, Eileen turned to me. "I'm confused," she said. "You used to be a musician. You even played drums for a while. How is it possible that you can't count to music?"

I shook my head. "I don't know. I think I just relied on my instincts. All this counting and walking…"

Three private lessons later, Tony promoted us back into the beginning class. Miraculously, we were no longer behind the others. All that personal attention had given us more confidence. We were swinging and swaying and switching hands, doing inside turns, outside turns, tuck turns, and sugar pushes.

"That is all for this evening, everybody," said Tony. "I see you next week. And please," he added, "come to Eymet for the dancing tomorrow. Some students from both classes will be there. It is very good to practice. And you can see some fireworks!"

I shivered.

Lesson 21

Bastille Day

JULY 14TH IS A SPECIAL DAY for the French. It celebrates the 1789 storming of the Bastille, a prison fortress in Paris that was known to contain a number of intellectual revolutionaries and a large cache of gunpowder. It turned out that the revolutionaries were somewhere else having a sandwich. But the gunpowder was useful.

This particular July 14th was a special day for the Americans. It was the day I discovered a hole in the roof of our barn. I had opened the door to toss in a bag of recyclables, and found a puddle of water on the floor. A tie beam that holds the walls together had come loose and was now hanging at a precarious angle. Daylight was visible through the roof. The puddle must have come from an overnight rain, allowed in by a shifting gable wall that was pulling the roof tiles apart.

If it's broke, do you have to fix it right away? This structure had lasted 400 years—another month or two wouldn't make much difference. I added the barn my mental to-do list and poured a glass of rosé.

Eileen, Sara, and I drove over to Eymet just before eight.

The dancing was scheduled for nine, and the fireworks for eleven-thirty. The idea was to enjoy our dinner first so we wouldn't cut into our dance time waiting in line for food.

Eymet (pronounced *AY-may*) is a charming bastide town built around a large arcaded square with an octagonal fountain. Fronting the square are restaurants, a wine shop, an antique store, and an English-speaking estate agent. The estate agent does a brisk business—properties in Eymet are catnip for Brits in search of second homes. The statistic we've heard is that one third of its property owners are British.

Les Américains are drawn to Eymet for a different reason. It has the only good Italian restaurant around for miles. The menu of the Restaurant Italien des Arcades offers 28 kinds of pizza, a wide range of pasta dishes, and ample carafes of good cheap wine. You don't know how much you miss Italian food until you've had a steady diet of duck confit for a month.

The owners are real Italians, not *imposteurs.* They hire family members to serve customers at a speed that would be unthinkable in French restaurants. Our waiter tonight was a seven-year-old boy with a black apron doubled up around his middle.

"Bonsoir, mesdames et monsieur," he said, a pencil behind one ear. "I am Vittorio. I can 'elp you?"

Eileen said: *"Une pizza margherita et une pizza caprese, s'il vous plaît."*

"Et un grand pichet de vin rouge," I added. Nothing says Bastille Day like a pitcher of Pecharmant and pizza.

Vittorio returned with two platters balanced on tiny hands. When we finished, he came back to take our credit card holding *la machine.* He could barely get his fingers around it. We managed to pay our bill without giggling.

We parked the car in a grassy field across the road from the bandstand. The music was playing and my blood pressure was rising. Sara had predicted that the picnic tables would be filled, so we brought our own *accoutrement:* picnic blankets, folding chairs, rosé, and wine glasses. These we carried in three large woven bags over our shoulders.

Up the road was a group of surly-looking teenagers, bunched together on the crest of a small bridge, smoking and talking in low tones as we approached. They were blocking the road.

I whispered to Sara and Eileen: "This could be trouble. Better let me handle it."

A well-muscled kid who appeared to be the ringleader walked up to me. His hair was shaved on the sides and moussed into high curls on top. A tarnished ring hung from his right ear. He wore a faded jeans jacket with the sleeves cut off, revealing several gang-style tattoos.

"Vous êtes Américains?" he said.

I looked at him, not answering.

"Do you know where the picnic area?" he said.

A girl emerged from the group. "Come this way," she said. "I show."

A young man with a cigarette and a gauzy mustache joined them. *"Oop-la!* Let me take the sacks."

They carried our picnic bags and led us through the park, chattering about Las Vegas and *The Simpsons* and Taylor Swift. When they were sure we had the best spot on the grass, they went back to help another group.

"Such polite kids," said Eileen. "Were you surprised?"

"Surprised? I was stunned. I thought they'd steal our bags and leave us lying on the ground with blood pouring from our fatal knife wounds."

"You wish," said Sara. "Then you wouldn't have to dance. Come on."

The dance floor was already a gyrating mass of humanity. Our favorite band, Les Touristes, blasted music from a raised stage. Thirty or so people, including a few we recognized from the advanced class, were doing a line dance. Sara tried to pull me out onto the floor. I yanked my hand back.

"I've never done a line dance!"

"It's easy!" she said. "Just go out there do what everybody else is doing."

"But I can't *tell* what they're doing!"

She left her fuddy-duddy dad and merged with the synchronizing dancers.

"This wasn't what we trained for," I explained to Eileen. It sounded like whining. The fact is, I was afraid to look foolish in front of my daughter and wife. I watched the dancers as closely as I could but wasn't able to make heads nor tails of the patterns.

The next song was a waltz. No good. Not our rhythm. I poured a glass of rosé for French courage.

The band struck up a reggae number with an up-tempo beat. Way too fast for West Coast Swing. We had to wait again.

Finally, Les Touristes launched into rousing version of *Mustang Sally,* complete with a strong bass line and snapping snare drum. Dancers rushed the floor. Eileen turned toward me with raised eyebrows.

I stepped back. "We can't dance *now!*" I said. "It's too crowded!" On stage, the band was cooking with hi-octane.

Ride, Sally, ride...

"Oh, come on," said Eileen, "this is one of the songs we worked on."

Ride, Sally, ride...

"Please? Can we wait for the next one?"

Ride, Sally, ride...

Eileen sighed. Les Touristes finished the song with a bang.

One of these lonely days—HUNH!

I'm gonna be wipin' those weepin' eyes.

As the last chords died the crowd went wild. The musicians took their bows and unplugged for a break. In the silence that followed, Eileen gazed at me with large, blue, innocent eyes. The corners of her mouth feigned sadness. With the accent of a French Ginger Rogers she sang:

> *Think of what you're losing*
> *By constantly refusing to dance with me—*
> *You'd be the idol of France with me!*

I answered in voice *à la* Fred Astaire:

> *I won't dance.*
> > *Don't ask me.*
> *I won't dance.*
> > *Don't ask me.*

She took my hand and swung me around. I sang:

> *I won't dance.*
> > *Why should I?*
> *I won't dance.*
> > *How could I?*
> *I won't dance.*
> > *Merci beaucoup!*

The crowd had moved beyond the dance floor to an open space marked off by cordons. A whistling noise cracked the air. Overhead a thousand stars exploded, sending showers of multicolored sparks down on uplifted faces. The fireworks had begun.

There are times when I look at Eileen and can't believe my luck. We married so young. There was no dancing, no honeymoon. Just back to work the next day. But we were the happiest people on earth. And as I looked at Eileen and then Sara, their smiling faces lighting up with every flash, I thought once again: I *am* lucky. Look what I got.

Every American knows the thrill of watching fireworks on the Fourth of July. The Fourteenth of July in France is not very different, but there's something about the Eymet version that recalls more innocent days. Suddenly we were seven years old—wide-eyed kids eating hot dogs and drinking lemonade in the park with our parents. It was lovely.

My only regret was that I couldn't bring myself to dance. My inner trooper had deserted me. Disappeared. Vanished. AWOL on the eve of battle.

Lesson 22

Bisous at the Bank

THE MORNING BROKE with a blast of sunshine and wall-to-wall blue skies. The birds were singing. The bees were humming. Eileen was busy in the kitchen, assembling a breakfast of ham-and-goat-cheese omelettes. The whole scene filled me with dread.

Today was banking day.

Up until now I had never attempted to complete more than the simplest of transactions. But this morning, in a single visit, I needed to correct our billing address, order a new checkbook, withdraw some cash, and arrange for a credit card.

The thought of banking was second only to the thought of dancing in its ability to send chills down my spine. Not only does it involve the serious matter of money, it requires a specialized vocabulary that I find confusing. For example, money is called *argent,* or silver, whereas change is called *monnaie,* as in money. Cash money isn't called *monnaie* at all, but *espèces,* and a checkbook is called a *carnet* instead of a *livre de chèques,* or book of checks, as you might expect.

And the numbers! Who came up with these? They skip

along predictably until they get up to seventy—then all hell breaks loose.

Eileen would quiz me: "Seventy-eight."

"Soixante-dix-huit," I would shoot back. Not seventy-eight, but sixty plus eighteen.

"Correct! Now, three hundred eighty."

"Trois cent quatre-vingt." Three hundred plus twenty times four. Apparently, the French have to learn to multiply before they can count.

"Okay…get this one right you can have the last piece of tarte tatin. Ten thousand nine hundred eighty-nine euros and ninety-nine cents."

Deep breath. *"Dix mille neuf cent quatre-vingt-neuf euros."*

"Et?"

"Et quatre-vingt-dix-neuf cents." At this point my left eye would start to twitch. Droplets of sweat would spring from my brow like rats deserting a ship. What is it with the French? It's as if they never anticipated counting beyond seventy. When they finally had to, they were forced to improvise. You can imagine their collective shrug: *"Ce n'est pas de notre faute."*

When you withdraw large amounts of cash at a French bank—*retirer de l'argent*—the teller doesn't count out bills from a drawer. She takes you over to a machine. There she extracts euros in small batches using a special magnetic card. Customers crane their necks to see how many batches you're taking out. This information quickly becomes a topic of conversation.

It was my turn to be a trooper. Today the bridge into

Bergerac was chock-a-block with traffic. I glanced at my watch. Eleven-fifteen. I needed to reach the Crédit Agricole before twelve, when it closes for lunch. The line of cars had slowed to the speed of *escargots*. Actually, that's not fair to escargots. In a race with a snail, the smart money would have been on the snail. I looked at my watch. It was now eleven-thirty.

Finally, the tempo picked up. At that very moment the taxi in front of me screeched to a halt. The driver rolled down the window and shouted something to a woman on the sidewalk. She came running over. He got out of the car, leaving his passengers inside.

"*Bonjour, Clarisse!*" he cried.

"*Bonjour, Marc. Ça va?*"

They traded kisses, or *bisous,* and conducted an animated discussion while dozens of drivers sat patiently behind us. I could only assume that this was normal in France. In the States, the other drivers would have hit level-three road rage by now, honking horns and making angry gestures from windows.

To my relief, the taxi resumed its progress. I parked the car and ran into the bank. Eleven-forty-five. There were seven customers in front of me. Would the doors close before I could reach the head of the line? Would my French be good enough to complete my transactions? I could already picture the teller stamping my withdrawal slip—INSUFFICIENT FRENCH. My pulse raced. Wet marks spread under my arms. I practiced my numbers. *Quarante et un.* Forty-one. *Deux cent soix-ante-treize.* Two hundred seventy-three. *Quatre cent cinquante.* Four hundred fifty.

One by one, as the customers reached the desk, they offered the teller polite greetings and double kisses. I panicked. Do I have to do this? I had no clue about the protocols that governed kissing in the bank. Surely an American would not be expected to participate. Would he?

I glanced to my left as a well-dressed young woman came through the double doors. She wore a tailored black suit with a white ruffled blouse and very high heels. She walked briskly in my direction, both arms extended. I turned around to see who she was looking at.

"*Monsieur Marty!*" she exclaimed, kissing me on both checks. "*C'est moi, Jacqueline!*"

I backed away involuntarily. Jacqueline? The sex-pot carpet installer? She looked different in business clothes. Older, more sophisticated. Her smile had the innocent sweetness of a poisoned petit four. She reached into a red leather handbag. Out came a book I'd written years ago on the subject of branding. My mind reeled. What were the odds of bumping into *anyone* with one of my books in France, much less someone I knew?

"I am learn English!" she said brightly.

My French numbers took a hike. My vocabulary dissolved into gibberish. All brain functions ceased. The only thing I managed to say was, "*Qu'est-ce qui se passe?*" What's going on?

I could feel the eyes of other customers boring into my back.

She launched into an all-French monologue, leafing through the book and holding up various pages. Her perfume was suffocating. I already couldn't think. Now I couldn't breathe. What was she saying? I heard the word *piscine,* swimming pool. Maybe I heard the word *rendez-vous,* appointment. She finished up with what sounded like a question, and stood there with an expectant look on her face. I was drowning. What do you say when a pretty girl floods you with unintelligible French?

"Uh…uh…*oui?*" I ventured. *"Bien sur?"*

"Formidable! Merci beaucoup! Au revoir." She tossed a gay wave as she spun around and walked into an office marked *Service de Prêt,* the loan department.

"Monsieur, c'est à vous," the teller said. I looked around, uncomprehending. *"Monsieur!"* she repeated, emphatically. *"C'EST—À—VOUS!"*

Yikes! My turn. The people behind me looked extremely annoyed.

"Um…*desolé,*" I said, head lowered. Jacqueline had crumpled my confidence like a ten-franc note, and now the teller was shredding it onto tiny little strips. I pulled out my cheat sheet. Let's see—how do I make a withdrawal?

"Je voudrais retirer de l'argent—non!—escargots—non!— ESPÈCES! I don't know. *Je ne sais pas!"*

The teller glared at me, waiting for some sense to appear. She softened when it dawned on her that she was not dealing with a competent adult.

"Monsieur," she said, articulating melodically, *"combien d'argent veux-tu?"* She was *tutoyer*ing me, using the word *tu* instead of *vous,* as if I were a child, or perhaps a favorite pet. I could feel my face redden. She was asking, How much money do you want?

"Je voudrais…je voudrais…quatre-dix cent cinquento?" Is that four hundred fifty? No, wait—that's Spanish. The hiss of whispers rose behind me. I tried again. *"Quatre cent deux-vingt-dix?"*

Somehow I managed to get through the transactions, but I'd been reduced to a quivering pool of perspiration. The doors were closing. I slipped out and angled through the covered market to Table du Marché. I needed to get my blood sugar up.

Stéphane, the restaurant's chef, placed a dish of perfectly seared scallops on the table in front of me, along with a large glass of rosé.

"Ça va?" His brow creased with concern.

I shook my head. *"Je ne sais pas."* I could barely taste the scallops. I took a sip of rosé and stared unseeing at the crowds in the marketplace.

What had Jacqueline said? What had I agreed to? What would Eileen think? Best not to go there.

Oh the *Vie!*

PETER SAID IT was my idea. Sara thought it was Christine's idea. Christine said it was Eileen's idea. Eileen thought it was Peter's idea. The main thing is that it was a *good* idea—a barbecue at the Johnsons' house for the boules players.

We divided up the work according to our skills. Sara would prepare the lion's share of the food, Peter would take charge of the tables and chairs, and Christine would bake some of her famous pies. Eileen and I would gather up the tableware, serve the wine, and help grill the meat. All the guests were invited to bring one or two of their favorite dishes.

By popular demand, duck burgers were back. Duck burgers for twenty, however, is what engineers in Silicon Valley might call a non-trivial task. It requires a half-day of shopping, a half-day of prepping, and a half-day of organizing food into Tupperware containers, trays, and serving bowls covered with plastic wrap.

On Wednesday morning, Sara and I drove to Bergerac. Hundreds of vendors had already set up around the church— fromagers, boulangers, vegetable sellers, vendors of fish, chicken, lamb, beef, and duck. Any local food you could want is there in spades.

Watching Sara work is inspiring. She shops with intent. First she walks the whole marketplace, making notes as she goes. Then, pencil in mouth, she picks out various kinds of produce to check for freshness, ripeness, and signs of damage. The vendors drop their usual banter when Sara approaches. She does a quick back-and-forth with each one before either buying or moving on. The only shoppers who earn similar respect are the older French women. They not only know the produce, but the prices. They'll comment sharply on any product that's a few cents over the average. Sara filled our bags with duck breast, onions, shallots, goat cheese, and butter lettuce. The baguettes would have to wait for the day of the event.

On Saturday, a few hours before the barbecue, Peter rumbled his tractor down the road. He loaded up our metal table and six metal chairs, then came back for the barbecue. With twenty people, we'd need two grills going at the same time.

The afternoon was sunny and warm with only a hint of a breeze. From Christine's flowers and herbs came a symphony of fragrances—rose, lavender, rosemary, thyme, and lemon balm. Peter had arranged the tables in a line in the gravel yard and covered them with checkered cloths. Pitchers of water punctuated the double rows of wine glasses, plates, and cutlery. The barbecues were fired up and standing off to the side. Sara brought the food and staged it on a table next to the barbecues.

They came bearing gifts. Jean-Pierre and Josette had made a tomato salad with feta cheese and sprigs of dried thyme. Anton and Sophie brought sliced melon and jambon sec splashed with Monbazillac. Robert and Jeannine had prepared a bowl of new potatoes sautéed in duck fat and sprinkled with rosemary and coarse sea salt. Gilbert and Michelle came with a large quiche lorraine. Jean-Cristophe and his wife, Marie, brought two more quiches. These were carried by their teenage kids, Clara and Cyril. Jean-Cristophe balanced a box of wine on his shoulder—a crisp Bergerac sec from his brother's vineyard.

"Who's that?" Eileen whispered to Christine.

"I'll introduce you." She pulled both of us over to Jean-Cristophe, a tallish man of about forty, fair-haired with blue eyes and a boyish smile.

"Jean-Cristophe, je vous présente nos voisins—our neighbors—Eileen and Marty." Then she turned to us. "Jean-Cristophe lives in Monbazillac. He's an electrician."

Eileen jumped. An electrician. Christine might have said "magician," or perhaps "prophet," considering the startled reaction she got. *"Enchanté, monsieur!"* said Eileen.

It wasn't just that Jean-Cristophe is tall and good looking, although he is. For Eileen he conjured visions of multiple appliances working together in mechanical harmony—toaster with tea kettle, washer with dryer, dishwasher with microwave. She tried to think of the French for "please come to my house immediately" without sounding like a cheap *putain.*

His gaze had shifted. *"Excusez-moi,"* he said, and hurried over to the barbecue area where Sara was placing pieces of buttered baguette on the grill.

"Vous êtes fatiguée. Allez-vous amuser," he said. "You're tired. Go have fun.

"Très gentil," said Sara, wiping her hands on her apron. She joined the three of us.

"Who's that?" she whispered to Eileen.

"Jean-Cristophe. He's an electrician."

Sara's eyes widened. "Oh—my—God."

We all nodded conspiratorially.

Eileen made a point of sitting between Jean-Cristophe and Marie. Sara sat next to Peter. I sat by Anna—an elegant German woman who had once been a ballet dancer—and her genial husband Jean-Claude. We passed platters of food up and down the tables while chatting up a storm in whatever languages we could manage. I rose from the table several times to fill fast-draining glasses with more Bergerac sec.

The duckburgers were delicious. The salads, the quiches, the potatoes—remarkable. The sun and the wine and the vibrant conversation had turned our cheeks pink. Christine brought out a tarte tatin, a cherry clafoutis, and, to a chorus of oohs and aahs, another of her famous lemon cheesecakes. The diners sampled every dish. The pies disappeared. *Nous avons bien mangé.* We had eaten well.

I stood up and raised my glass. *"La vie est belle!"*

Everyone shouted back, *"La vie est belle!"* and clinked their glasses.

Peter said: *"Vie.* That reminds me—the *eau de vie."* Georges had given Peter a bottle of illegal eau de vie—water of life—as a gift on his last visit. This particular moonshine was made from plums and had an alcohol content of around 90 percent. It was distilled insanity. Peter ran into the house to grab it.

He came out and poured everyone a thimbleful of the stuff and strode to head of the table.

"I'd like to propose a toast to Sara, who worked so hard to make this barbecue possible." Sara was slumped in a plastic chair. Her cheeks were flushed—they had started out rosy but were now bright red.

"Santé!" said everyone, downing their drinks. Peter poured a second, slightly larger, glass for Sara.

"You deserve it, young lady. Good job."

Sara smiled at Peter and took a sip of Georges's elixir.

When the guests were gone and the sun had set, we helped the Johnsons clear the tables. We packed our tableware in boxes and brought them home. The rest of the cleaning could wait.

Back on the terrace at Le Rêve, we found Sara staring vacantly into the distance.

"Sara?" said Eileen. *"Ça va?"*

"Oui, maman," she said. She turned towards me. *"La mer est très bleue aujourd'hui."*

I said, "The sea is blue? What are you talking about?"

"*Quoi, papa?*"

"What do you mean, the sea is blue today? It's night."

"*Je ne comprehends pas.*" She looked at me, then at her mother, brows furrowed. "*Quand partons-nous?*"

"She wants to know when we're leaving," said Eileen. We had planned to go to Bordeaux in the morning.

"*Je dois ranger ma serviette de plage,*" said Sara.

Eileen and I looked at each other. I went to the bookcase and pulled out a dictionary. A *serviette de plage* is a beach towel. She wants to pack her beach towel? Bordeaux doesn't have a beach. It's miles inland.

"Sweetie, we're not going to the beach," Eileen said. "We're going to Bordeaux. You can pack in the morning."

"*Maman, parle français!*"

Just then I had an epiphany. "It's the eau de vie. It must have scrambled her brain. She can only speak French."

"Really?" said Eileen. She tried to remember the French for "go to bed." *Allez au lit.*

"*Ma petite, allez au lit,*" she said, placing a hand on Sara's forehead. "*Tu es très, très fatigué. Je vais te réveiller demain matin.*"

"*D'accord, maman,*" said Sara. She turned mechanically and walked into her bedroom.

In our own bedroom, Eileen and I finally turned off the lights. What had happened? Why couldn't Sara speak English? Should we take her to the emergency hospital? Was this a temporary affliction or would she be French forever?

There was a knock on our door. I opened it. Sara stood there wearing a light blue sun dress and a big straw hat. Her pink suitcase was packed by her side.

"*Je suis prête. Allons-y?*"

Eileen put her arm around her. "*Tu es fatiguée, ma petite. Recouch-toi.*" She walked Sara back to her room.

Early the next morning Eileen and I sat at the breakfast table. We needed coffee after a sleepless night. The door burst open. Sara bounced into the kitchen, apparently revived from the rigors of the previous day.

"*Bonjour, mes parents!*"

Our hearts hit the floor.

Then she said, brightly, "Should I make you two some breakfast?"

We jumped up and hugged our English-speaking daughter like there was no tomorrow. Oh, the *vie,* the wonderful *vie.*

DUCK BURGERS

The signature dish of Le Rêve. I find grinding the duck and forming the patties for a triple batch of burgers a soothing way to get over jet lag. It's comforting to know there's an ample supply in the freezer. If you don't have a meat grinder, you can cut the duck breasts into one inch pieces and pulse them in a food processor until the meat is the texture of hamburger. —*Sara*

4 tablespoons butter
2 medium shallots, finely chopped
2 one-pound magret duck breasts, passed through
    a meat grinder or food processor
Salt and pepper to taste
2 twelve-inch baguettes
1/2 cup onion jam (see recipe below)
6 ounces fresh goat cheese

1. Melt butter in a small skillet and set aside half in a small bowl for buttering baguettes. Add shallots to skillet and sauté over medium heat until tender and translucent. Let cool.

2. In a large bowl combine shallots, duck, salt, and pepper. Form into 6 patties. Place patties on a parchment lined sheet

tray, and place tray in freezer to chill until firm, about 20 minutes.

3. Meanwhile, heat grill to high. Slice baguettes horizontally and brush insides with reserved butter. Cut each baguette into thirds to form 3 "buns."

4. Grill patties until medium rare, 4–6 minutes per side. Grill baguette sections until just toasted. Serve patties on baguettes with the onion jam and goat cheese.

Serves 6

CONFIT D'OIGNON
Onion Jam

We keep this on hand especially for duck burgers, but it's also good combined with goat cheese in baked stuffed vegetables, or as a condiment with other roast meats or cheese. —*Sara*

    6 large red onions, thinly sliced
    3 tablespoons vegetable or olive oil
    1/3 cup balsamic vinegar

Heat oil in a large, high-sided skillet over medium-low heat. Add onions and cover. Cook, stirring occasionally, until onions are tender and beginning to turn golden, about 15 minutes. Add balsamic vinegar and continue to cook, uncovered, stirring occasionally until onions are a rich brown, 20–30 minutes. If during cooking onions begin to stick to the pan, add a few tablespoons water (or wine) and stir with a wooden spoon to dislodge any brown bits. Store, refrigerated, in an airtight container for up to 10 days.

Makes 2 cups

TARTE AU CITRON À LA CHRISTINE
Christine's Famous Lemon Cheesecake

Our neighbor Christine is a genius at sniffing out great recipes from British newspapers. This one, described as "easy, peasy, lemon squeezy," is totally brilliant. Five ingredients and no baking! To adjust the level of sweetness, you can add or subtract from the amount of condensed milk—it's pretty foolproof. Chris likes to present it garnished with a graphic pattern of thinly sliced limes on top. Raspberries or toasted sliced almonds look lovely, too. —*Sara*

    8 ounces gingersnap cookies, finely ground
    5 ounces unsalted butter, melted
    16 ounces mascarpone cheese
    Finely grated zest of 2 lemons

Juice of 3–4 lemons, depending on desired tartness
2/3 cup sweetened condensed milk
(about half a 14-ounce can)

1. In a medium bowl combine gingersnap crumbs and melted butter. Press evenly into the bottom and sides of a 9-inch tart tin. Set aside.

2. Using a hand-held or standing mixer on low, combine remaining ingredients until smooth. Pour into reserved crust, smoothing top with a spatula. Refrigerate at least 4 hours or overnight before serving.

Serves 8

☞ Photos and printable versions are at **www.beginningfrench.com**

Lesson 24

Liberté, Égalité, Électricité

YOU CAN'T HAVE a free and equal society without electricity. If your washer and dryer don't work at the same time, you're not free. You're imprisoned by your laundry. Your shirts turn into straightjackets. Your underwear holds you hostage. You can't wash a second load until the first load is dry, which doubles your working time. And if your washer and dryer are the smaller European type, like ours, you need to run more loads. You're tethered to your appliances for the duration—usually a whole day.

In the society we call our family, each of us has a different responsibility. I gravitate toward problems emanating from the outside. Sara, whenever she visits, takes care of the kitchen. Eileen handles home maintenance, making sure that everything runs smoothly—the laundry, the housecleaning, the gardening. Normally we see these as equally weighted roles, but they quickly become lopsided when appliances fight back.

Today, while Eileen swore at the washer and dryer, Sara battled the kitchen appliances. She couldn't run the hand mixer and the electric oven at the same time. Or the microwave and the toaster. Or the coffee maker and the kettle. Cooking takes timing. If your soufflé batter is ready for the oven but the oven shuts off, your batter sinks while you sort it out.

I called up Christine to see if she might intercede with Jean-Cristophe. Could she possibly persuade him to take a look? Two hours later she called back with good news. Next Thursday at six o'clock.

The pope himself could not have expected a better reception. The three of us were waiting at the kitchen door wearing our best line-dried clothes. Christine was there to translate French to English and English to French. Peter was there to translate Technology to English.

Jean-Cristophe arrived. *"Vous avez un problème?"* he said, his sparkling blue eyes sweeping the kitchen for an electrical box.

"There's a box here in the kitchen," I said, pointing up, "and another box in the salon. There's also a box in the master suite." Christine translated this.

"Oh, la la," he said.

"And every time we turn on too many appliances, the electricity goes out." I showed him the box in the salon with the black button.

He shook his head. *"Vous avez un système triphasé,"* he said.

"Is that bad?" I asked.

He pushed out his lower lip and shrugged his shoulders.

He took a screwdriver from his tool belt and removed the circuit breakers from the box in the kitchen. He turned them around to look at the wiring.

"*Votre système est déséquilibré. Trop d'appareils sur une phase.*"

"Your system is unbalanced," said Christine.

I wasn't sure if I should be offended.

"You have too many appliances running on one phase."

"That's what I was wondering," said Peter. "Ask him if we should change the system to monophase."

Christine put the question to Jean-Christophe.

"*Pas nécessaire,*" he said. "I fix."

We left him alone to do his magic, and when we checked back a half-hour later he announced: "*J'ai terminé.* Your kitchen work." He turned on the oven, the toaster, the microwave, the dishwasher, and finally the coffee maker. He ducked into the laundry room and started the washer and dryer. Everything worked and the lights stayed on. The mood was, in a word, electric.

In France it's traditional to kiss your neighbors when you part. Eileen was the first to plant one on Jean-Cristophe's heroic, blushing cheek. "*Merci beaucoup,*" she said, "*vous êtes un rock star.*"

The kitchen working, I could now turn my attention to other items on the list. The road, for example. Dennis Henderson had spent thousands of euros to pave our *chemin rural* with calcaire, a powdered limestone that made the road leading to the hamlet look fabulous. But there were two small problems.

Problem one: When it was dry and windy, white dust blew everywhere—into our house, our car, our hair—everywhere.

Problem two: When it rained, the calcaire turned to gooey cement, sticking to our tires and glomming onto our shoes. It dried as hard as rock and wouldn't come off.

My solution was to forge a three-nation deal. The Americans would pay for the road, just as Dennis had done, but this time only the materials. Philippe, a French farmer who used the road to access his fields, would perform the labor using his own machinery and manpower. The Brits—Peter and Christine—would supervise the project in my absence. The goal was to finish the job before the rains came.

The next item on my list was to replace our caretakers, who weren't taking much care at all. Margaret Snyder ran a competent house-cleaning operation, but the gardening and pool staff created more problems than they solved. They planted shrubs where they would obstruct the view, replaced gravel with the wrong size and color, left furniture outside to rust in the rain.

We had just met Jan and Derek Goacher, a lovely couple from Cornwall, at the night market in Creysse. They had married on a Sunday, moved to France on Monday, and started their maintenance business on Tuesday. Jan was in charge of household projects, and Derek the pool and the garden. We've yet to find something he can't fix. They were practical, reliable, and efficient. I signed them up to take over.

Finally, the barn. Okay, the building had weathered 400 years of existence without us, but I didn't want it to fall down now—not on my watch. I set up a meeting with Georges to see what he could do. He suggested we dismantle the gable end of the barn stone by stone, then build it back square, reattaching the tie beam and replacing part of the roof. For a few euros more he would throw in a window to admit some light into the darkest corner.

Owning a 400-year-old house is a relationship. As with all relationships, you have to pay attention to it. You can't take it for granted and expect it to last. Whereas some kinds of aging are charming and artistic, other kinds are fatal. Rural France is littered with abandoned houses—houses left for dead, houses past the point of no return. If you look, you'll find ruins for sale at ridiculously low prices. But they can never be restored. Their relationships have failed.

With Jean-Cristophe on our team, along with Philippe, Georges, the Goachers, and the Johnsons, we now felt better about our chances of survival. We'd had so many problems. On the other hand, we'd gotten so much help from our new friends and neighbors.

The summer was almost over. There was time for one more celebration.

Lesson 25

The Last Supper

LOOKING BACK, it had been a summer of progress. There had been no boiler explosions. No pool contaminations. No major plagues. We had gained the acceptance of the boules group, discovered the joys of night markets, and cracked the code for duck burgers. We had even learned to dance—after a fashion.

Okay, maybe the barn had a few problems and the electric circuits occasionally failed. But we now had a support team to address those issues. We felt a victory lap was warranted.

Our friends David and Susan had been entertaining a steady flow of guests all summer, so our schedules had never meshed. But now the Stuarts were free. We wanted to demonstrate our progress, to reassure them that their work on our behalf had not been in vain. And we wanted to express the deep sense of gratitude we felt for all their encouragement and advice. What better way than with a festive French dinner, Stuart style?

"Stuart style" is our shorthand for a type of hospitality marked by grace, wit, and authentic charm. The Stuarts make it look easy. And, as everyone knows, making anything look easy is anything *but.* It takes careful planning, hard work, and a *soupçon* of luck.

Sara got started on a menu. Eileen and I got started on the guest list. Who else to invite? Our table seats eight, and with the Stuarts we were already five. We decided to ask one more couple.

"Remember the Americans we met at the frame shop in Bergerac?" I said to Eileen.

"Yes! Last summer. He's an architect and she's a project manager at Google. They spend summers here."

"Bryan and Karen. They were picking up a hand-tinted map of France. We had a great conversation about cartography, travel, design, art, and France. We had lunch together. We traded emails."

"I think the Stuarts would enjoy them," said Eileen. "Let's see if they're available."

I found their email address and composed a brief invitation. Twenty minutes later they accepted.

Sara was pumped. Her goal was to make this dinner the culinary experience of a lifetime. Earlier in the summer she'd perfected a version of lobster Thermidor that knocked our socks off. Liver, roe, and lobster juice, when combined with a sherry-infused Béchamel, became a little piece of heaven under the heat of the broiler. This recipe would form the main course.

Dinner would begin innocently, a crisp green salad dressed in shallot-lemon vinaigrette. Next would come a startling snow pea and green bean mélange borrowed from the œuvre of Yotam Ottolenghi. Potatoes Anna would follow—layered slices of white potato in butter, baked into a creamy galette. Just when the guests believed that no meal could get any better, the lobster Thermidor would destroy that notion. And after a brief recess to regain our composure, a light tarte au citron paired with espresso. The wines would move effortlessly from champagne to sauvignon blanc to Bergerac sec and to pinot noir.

The day before the dinner, Sara prepped the side dishes. The aromas in the kitchen were already giving off hints of greatness.

"Have we forgotten anything?" said Eileen.

"I think we're set," said Sara. "Most of the food is either ready to eat or ready to cook. We just need to pick up six lobsters from Leclerc."

We realize that we're not the Stuarts. Not yet. But there's one thing you can say about *les Américains:* we work well together. Our can-do attitude and division of labor guarantees a minimum-viable product. That's technology-speak for "we do a good-enough job." We can juggle a massive number of variables because there's always a Plan B. We constantly scan the horizon for new problems, possible surprises, and unknown unknowns. This level of vigilance gives us a certain confidence. Which is why we weren't prepared for what happened next.

The guests were due in five hours. Sara and I drove to Leclerc to pick up lobsters. We made our way through the crowded aisles to the live crustacean section. We couldn't believe our eyes. The tank was empty! Only two scrawny lobsters, listless in their thick rubber bands.

"What?" cried Sara. "That's impossible. They *always* have lobsters here."

She marched over to the seafood manager. *"Ou sont les homards?"* she said, her voice rising slightly.

"Ils sont partis," he said, as if the lobsters got bored and set off for greener pastures.

"They left?" I said. "Where'd they go?"

He shrugged. *"Sais pas."*

I turned to Sara. "There's a big Intermarché down the street. Let's go."

We bought the two anemic lobsters as insurance, then drove down the street. The man behind the seafood counter told us they didn't carry homards at Intermarché. Had we tried Leclerc?

"Wait," said Sara. "Isn't there another Leclerc in the old town?"

Bergerac has a complicated system of streets in the older section. We ended up driving around for an hour before we found the store.

"Thank God!" I said.

We ran to the fish section.

No lobster tank.

"Allez au poissonier," said the seafood manager. He offered directions to a nearby fish shop, miming indecipherable hieroglyphics with his hands.

The clock was ticking. We managed to find the fish shop in only three-quarters of an hour, an improvement over our last time. It was now three in the afternoon. Just as we walked up to the shop, the proprietor pulled down a big metal door. *"Plus de poisson,"* he said. No more fish. Hope was now receding like a wave on a stony shore.

"Hey!" Sara cried. "Isn't there a huge Leclerc just north of Bergerac?"

I stopped her right there. "Okay, let's think about this. Only three hours to go, and you still have to cook. Shouldn't we come up with an alternate plan? Maybe another great recipe for the main course?"

"Dad, you don't understand. You can change a lot of things on a menu. You can substitute one entrée for another, one appetizer for another, one dessert for another. But you can't change the main course without changing everything else. All the flavors and textures are interdependent."

She was right. I wouldn't ask Frank Lloyd Wright if perhaps a small fountain wouldn't work just as well at Fallingwater. I wouldn't ask Beethoven to swap out the *da-da-da-DUH* in the Fifth Symphony with a catchy *bippity-boppity-boo*. I wouldn't ask Van Gogh to replace the stars in "The Starry Night" with, let's say, some nice fluffy clouds. Lobster Thermidor is what Sara planned, and lobster Thermidor is what we would serve.

We drove north. The Leclerc outside of town was so large that it straddled the street. We entered the south building and were told that the seafood store was in the north building. Only two hours to go. We ran to the back of the store and —there it was, big as life: a lobster tank with four healthy lobsters.

The kitchen table at Le Rêve was a picture of French elegance. Eileen had arranged our best dishes and flatware on blue cotton placemats and matching cotton napkins. The wine glasses sparkled like diamonds. Bottles of champagne and chardonnay sat chilling in a shabby-chic metal bucket. Warm candlelight reflected off polished surfaces.

Sara raced the clock to finish the lobster, sliding trays in and out of ovens and slamming doors. Only fifteen minutes to go.

The phone rang. It was Karen.

"Listen," she said. "Marty. I'm so sorry. We'll have to have to cancel tonight. Bryan isn't feeling well."

"Oh no," I said, trying to hide the true state of my panic. "Is it the flu? A summer cold?"

"Well, frankly, he's a little depressed. He just lost an important project to a large firm. I'm afraid he wouldn't be very good company."

"Karen, are you sure? Can't you come anyway? It might be good therapy to socialize. We can help put everything into perspective. We've all been there."

"Well…I don't know." She paused, then put her hand over the phone. She came back: "Bryan says okay. But we'll be about thirty minutes la—."

The phone went dead. The lights flickered. A wail came from the kitchen.

"D-A-D! The broiler went off! I can't finish the lobster without the broiler!"

I ran in. Eileen and Sara were looking at the half-baked lobsters in the oven.

"Can you microwave it for the last part?"

Sara put her hands on her hips and stared at me.

"No. Okay. I get it. What else?"

"Nothing," she said. "We're stuck."

We stood around wondering what to do. The front gates squeaked and the Stuarts appeared in the courtyard.

"Yoo-hoo! Americans!" Susan called cheerily.

As if on cue, the broiler came on. Sara went back to work, trying to save the lobsters from a soggy, sorry fate.

Eileen met the Stuarts at the door and quickly took them through to the terrace. Outside I poured each of us a *cocktail de la maison*—a glass of champagne with a splash of chambord, to serve with warm gougères.

"Cheers," said Eileen. "Karen and Bryan said they'll be a little late." She paused. "Be nice to Bryan. He's had a business reversal today and may need some cheering up."

The Stuarts made sympathizing sounds as they sipped their drinks.

The gates squealed again. Bryan stood in the gateway, swaying slightly, arms full of bottles—champagne, wine, pastis, and whiskey. Karen stood behind him with a nervous smile.

"Is this the place?" he said. "Some view!" He showed no signs of depression. If anything, he was ebullient. The social therapy seemed to be working already. "I brought a few things to drink!"

At Bryan's suggestion, I fixed a small pastis for each of us. Normally, you would expect a few uncomfortable lulls in any pre-dinner conversation, but Bryan filled them handily with stories from past parties.

"I was at Philip Johnson's 90th birthday. The famous architect. Some of us went swimming. I felt so embarrassed at dinner."

"Why?" said Eileen.

"I got a little drunk and peed in the pool."

"Oh, hey," said Eileen. "Accidents happen. Lots of us have peed in the pool."

"From the diving board?" he said.

Stunned silence, then tentative chuckles from me and Eileen. The Stuarts laughed politely, unsure if this was what passed for American humor. Karen was quietly turning red.

It seemed like a good opportunity to change the scene. I

called everyone to dinner and poured us all glasses of chardonnay. Sara brought out the entrée. The conversation, in the meantime, had grown louder and more animated.

Halfway through the meal I shot a glance at Sara. She'd barely touched her lobster Thermidor. She looked at me and could see what I was thinking. It wasn't that the dinner was *bad,* but it wasn't inspiring. In fact, it was below the standard of Sara's everyday cooking.

I can always tell when Eileen is upset in a social situation. She gets busy. "Excuse me," she said. "I'm going out to get the candles from the terrace." She kicked me under the table. I followed her out.

"Bryan is cooked," she said.

"Cooked?"

"He's whacked."

"What?"

"He's blotto! Drunk as a skunk! Can't we do something?"

We went back to the kitchen to find our American friend holding forth on the state of European architecture.

"The French don't have a goddamn clue about Modernism," he sputtered. "And look at the Brits! I mean, really. *Pickles?"* His voice was growing shrill.

"The Gherkin," corrected David, referring to the glassy green skyscraper by Sir Norman Foster.

"Pickles, gherkins, cucumbers." Bryan got up and turned to me. "What else do you have to drink?"

Sara pushed him down in his chair. "Does anyone know

the lyrics to *Boum?*"

Eileen rushed to join her, and the two sang a spontaneous duet, dancing comically around the table.

> *Mais... BOUM!*
>> *Quand notre cœur fait boum*
>> *Tout avec lui dit boum*
>>> *et c'est l'amour qui s'eveille*
> *BOUM!...*

They ended on one knee with their arms spread like Charles Trenet. Bryan stood unsteadily to lead the applause. He then went to the cabinet above the sink and found a mostly empty bottle of gin. He transferred the gin to his wine glass.

"Got any vermoose?" he asked, weaving in place.

Karen caught him by the arm. "Okay, hon, time to go." She made apologetic gestures to the rest of us while Bryan drained the contents of his glass. We said our goodbyes and kissed each other's cheeks.

"All this kissing," he said. "I'm getting *horny!*"

The moment they were out the door, the Stuarts rose to leave. "All good things must, you know," said David, smiling graciously. "Thank you so much for inviting us. Such a lively evening."

"You Americans know how to party," teased Susan.

When they left, we shut the door and started clearing the table.

"What do you think?" said Sara. "Pretty good, considering."

"Not exactly Stuart style," I said, "but passable, right?"

Eileen said nothing.

The next morning we met in the kitchen. Sara was the first to broach the subject.

"So tell me, honestly. Bad dinner—or worst dinner ever?"

I sighed.

Eileen said, "We've done better, that's for sure. I felt like the line judge at the Tennis Match from Hell. You and Sara kept trying to redirect the conversation and Bryan kept smashing words out of bounds. *Quel nightmare!*"

We immediately sent an apology to David and Susan. Susan emailed back: "We had a delightful time. We haven't laughed so hard in ages." How like our friends to put everything in the best possible light.

But. We'd set out to create an evening of sumptuous food and clever conversation. We failed. Everything that could go wrong did go wrong. First the lobster crisis, then the oven outage, and finally the human time bomb who only agreed to come at my insistence. In Silicon Valley this is called a cascading failure—a system-wide collapse in which one problem triggers another, then another, and so forth, until the whole enterprise crashes to the ground. *BOUM!*

Sara packed her bags for New York; Eileen and I started closing the house for the winter. We hauled our luggage to the car. When we locked the gates I had the strangest sensation. I felt physically ill—as if we were abandoning a helpless child. The nausea only faded when we boarded the plane to California and I could turn my thoughts back to business.

Lesson 26

Pugs in Paris

JUNE ROLLED AROUND and vacation planning began in earnest. My biggest challenge was arranging my client work so I could duck out for a couple of months. This didn't mean I could leave my work behind. It always comes with me.

Eileen's biggest challenge was getting our two pugs on the plane. There was Boodles, a fawn female with a strong fashion sense (true), and Bingo, her best friend in the world—male, black, and humorously vocal. We can leave them with a house sitter for three or four weeks at a time, but eight weeks would amount to cruel and unusual punishment. Pugs live to sit on their owners' laps. Depriving them of said laps is pure torture from a pug's point of view.

Normally we would travel to France via London. From there it's a short flight to Bergerac, and then a ten-minute car ride to the house. But UK policy is less than pet-friendly to travelers from the US—Americans have to start their paperwork six months in advance, and finish the process in the UK before traveling onward. The sensible plan was to bring the dogs straight into pet-loving Paris. From there we would catch the TGV, or "train of great speed," down to Bordeaux. In Bordeaux we could rent a car and drive the ninety minutes to Le Rêve.

One little hurdle remained. The matter of canine health certificates, otherwise known as the United States Interstate and International Certificates of Health Examination for Small Animals, issued by the Department of Agriculture.

It works like this. No more than ten days before your departure, you submit the aforementioned form and a rabies certificate, both signed by your vet, to the nearest USDA office. During that period they process your request and send back a signed and stamped Endorsement for International Export. It all works seamlessly until something goes wrong. And something always goes wrong.

Eileen FedExed the forms to arrive exactly ten days before our plane was scheduled to take off. Days went by. Then more days. Finally we got a call from a man at the Agriculture Department.

"We got your package," he said, "but there was nothing but a cover sheet listing the contents."

"Not possible," said Eileen. "I sent the papers and the check myself."

"Well, they're not here."

No stranger to bureaucratic run-ins, Eileen was ready. "I scanned everything. Should I send it to you?"

He paused. "Let me look around. I'll call you back in a few."

Two days later he rang. "No problem," he said. "Found 'em.

One of our people dropped a stack of papers on the floor and got them mixed up. We'll send you everything tomorrow."

Now, we would never advocate skipping the whole nerve-wracking process and sneaking your dogs into another country without their paperwork. But it must be said that in all the times we've flown with our pets, no one has asked for their papers.

They *have* questioned our intentions for taking the dogs in the first place. On this particular trip, a security agent grew suspicious as she rifled through Eileen's carry-on bag.

"What's all this stuff?" she said, eyes narrowing.

"It's for the dogs," said Eileen.

"All of it?" She opened a small Tupperware container. "What's this?"

"Peanut butter. For the dogs' pills."

"Peanut butter is a gel."

"I'd say it's more of a paste," said Eileen with an innocent expression.

"I'm sorry, we can't allow—"

"Please. Do I look like the Peanut Butter Bomber?"

Passengers in line started to giggle. Two men with badges rushed out to escort Eileen to another room. Two others grabbed the pugs.

"Where are you taking them?" I cried.

Over his shoulder, one of the agents said: "To the X-ray machine. These dogs could be stuffed with explosives."

"They just look like that!" I yelled.

Eventually, wife and pugs were cleared. We were free to board the plane as a family. The pugs were perfect passengers.

Our 747 touched down the next morning. The air in Paris was cool, the sky a patchwork of cotton puffballs against a bright blue background. Our taxi driver unloaded the luggage onto the sidewalk near the Gare Montparnasse. I put Bingo on his leash.

I looked around. No Eileen. No Boodles. They'd been swallowed by the crowd around the train station. I shoved an extra ten-euro note in the taxi driver's hand. "Could you watch our bags for a second? *Garder vos bagages, s'il vous plaît?*"

On the sidewalk ahead I heard the clear voice of an English speaker.

"Look, Boodles! The Eiffel Tower!" Boodles was cantilevered forward in the outstretched hands of my wife, all the better to see Europe's most iconic monument. More than a few passersby turned to see where Boodles was looking. They seemed to notice the Eiffel Tower for the first time. I ran up.

"Why are you doing that?" I said. I glanced nervously at our luggage.

"It's on her bucket list."

I turned Eileen around to go back. Boodles craned her neck towards the tower.

"What else is on her bucket list?" I said.

"She wants to walk down the Champs Elysée in a rhinestone collar."

"Jeez, anything else?"

"She wants to have a Kir at the Café de Flore.

I gave her a look.

"Well, actually, she wants *me* to have a Kir."

"And what does Bingo want?"

"He just wants Boodles to be happy."

We pulled our dogs and baggage into a sidewalk café, leaving our bags with the waiter. We had a full hour before our train departed for Bordeaux. A feature of French life is that dogs—at least the small ones—are expected to sit in café chairs like adults. We each took a seat at a table for four. The waiter immediately brought a water bowl for Boodles and Bingo.

"Ah, mignon," he said, cupping Boodles's pushed-in face in his palm. *"Avez-vous choisi?"*

I turned to Eileen: "Does Boodles want you to have a Kir?"

"Don't be silly. It's still morning."

"Well, I need one."

We sipped our drinks in a jetlagged fog, gazing at the passing parade known as Paris. An American couple strolled by.

"Shhh! Don't say a word," whispered Eileen.

They'd stopped just beyond us and were now taking photos with their iPhones.

"Isn't that wonderful!" said the woman. The pugs were sitting politely on their red wicker chairs, a drink in front of each.

"They're so French!" said the man, waggling his fingers at Boodles and Bingo.

Thus began the best summer of their lives.

A Perfect Day

WE REACHED LE RÊVE and the dogs jumped out of the car to a freedom they'd never known. They took off down the *chemin rural,* tails curling, feet flying. France would be a whole new experience, a feast for the senses.

These aren't your average stay-at-home pugs. They're action pugs. They had become agility stars, and they loved to show off their tricks. In the Dordogne they learned how to behave well in fine restaurants, entertain children at the brocantes, and forage for frites under the tables at the night markets.

Boodles had taught herself a trick Houdini would have appreciated. She'd lie in the sun outside the kitchen door, seemingly asleep, with one eye on the house. When we were sufficiently preoccupied, she'd tiptoe around the back and out through the hedge. By the time we'd realize she was gone, she'd have been sitting on Peter's lap for an hour helping him work. "Have you met my new dog?" he'd say, appearing at our door with Boodles in his arms.

Three weeks into the summer, I stood at the head of a conference room at Les Vigiers, a 16th-century chateau between

Duras and Bergerac. It was now a luxury hotel with a 27-hole golf course and two restaurants.

Sitting before me were nine professionals who had traveled halfway around the world to spend five days redesigning their businesses. Two came from Australia, one from Canada, one from Finland, two from Spain, one the UK, and two more from the Republic of Georgia. This was a chance to work with talented people I only knew as readers. The grand finale on the afternoon of Day Five would be a fête in the courtyard of Le Rêve, catered by none other than Chef Sara.

The workshop went well. The participants brought passion and creativity to their projects. Everyone learned from everyone else. We labored seriously during the day, and at night we laughed ourselves silly over dinner. We went for pizza in Eymet, duck in Duras, and salade chèvre chaud in Thénac. I couldn't believe how the group had bonded.

Whenever Eileen and I tell people about our little house, we emphasize that it's not really a house. It's a structure. It takes all our resourcefulness just to keep it standing. It looks good in photos because you can't take a bad picture of France. But photos don't show the power outages, the problematic plumbing, the squadrons of bugs, or the cracks that signify something less innocent than charm.

But when I came through the gates on the day of the fête, all of those thoughts vanished. The large, leafy tree in the courtyard reached up to a sky so blue it would make a robin blush. The shutters and doors wore a fresh coat of lavender paint. The old stone buildings framed golden fields and lush green forests that seemed to go on forever. Flowers brightened the boundaries, and two young olive trees stood proudly in oversized pots against the barn. The pool, for once, was clear and blue and inviting, and the laurel hedge at the back appeared to have been trimmed with a straightedge. On the horizon of the courtyard, under the big ash tree, were three tables set with dishes, cutlery, and wine glasses. A soft warm breeze ruffled the edges of a pressed white tablecloth. Next to the tables sat the galvanized metal tub with chilled bottles of champagne and white wine.

"What do you think?" said Eileen, wiping her hands on her apron.

I was dumbfounded. I wasn't expecting a transformation of this magnitude. What an effort this must have taken! I'd envisioned a casual barbecue to send my guests on their merry way. Instead, I got the reunion scene from *French Kiss.* My heart soared.

"Wow," was all I could say. Was this really my life?

The Australians arrived first, snapping photos of the view and the house and the tables under the tree. The Georgians came next, bringing more bottles of wine. The Spaniards, the Canadian, the Brit, and the Finn quickly followed. They couldn't stop talking about the picture-perfect setting and the beautiful weather.

Eileen and Sara poured white sangria made from Bergerac sec and sparkling water. Glasses swirled with the colors of summer—peaches, raspberries, and citrus slices soaked in Monbazillac wine.

Out came the food. An heirloom tomato salad. Blanched fava beans and haricots verts sautèed with garlic and tossed with chopped tarragon and crumbles of semi-aged goat cheese. Two girolles-and-cream tarts made with local mushrooms sautéed in butter with garlic and parsley. A salmon filet, made from a recipe by Sara's friend Lynn, covered with coarse and smooth Dijon and sprinkled with capers.

The combination was magical.

One of the Spaniards dabbed the corner of his mouth and turned to me. "Tell me, does the Tour de France ever come through here?" Six or seven heads bobbed up.

"Funny you should ask," I said. "This'll be the first year." I stood and pointed toward Monbazillac. "Right up there." They craned their necks, straining to see the race in their mind's eye. "We're pretty excited about it."

As the eating wound down, the entertainment portion of the afternoon began. A delegate from the Republic of Georgia had asked about the dogs.

"Do they have tricks?" he said.

"*Do* they!" said Eileen.

She walked around to an open space in front of the tables, pugs heeling obediently.

"Invités d'honneur, je vous présente Madame Boodles et Monsieur Bingo."

The dogs sat down side by side in front of her, faces turned upward. They spun to the left and then to the right. They rolled over in unison. Bingo danced on his hind legs. Boodles played dead with one eye open.

"Say *bonjour* to your guests." They waved with their right paws. Everyone waved back.

"Monsieur Bingo is *exceptionnel,*" she said. "He does interviews. Bingo, can you say 'I love you' to your fans?"

"I ruv you!" he said, with a clarity that rivaled many rock stars.

"Can you sing like a bird?"

"B-r-r-r-r-r-l," he chirped melodically.

"Can you give us a rebel yell?

"W-r-a-a-a-o-o-o-a-a-h-r!" he cried loudly, his voice distorting like an overtaxed amplifier.

An Australian stood to applaud, tipping over her chair. The others cheered. Eileen spread her arms and Bingo leapt into them. She curtseyed to the crowd and left the stage. The table shook with laughter.

Over strawberry pie with chantilly, the guests spoke excitedly about their new business goals. They compared the politics and economics of their respective countries. They talked about travel, food, and wine. They shared their plans for their remaining time in France. They raised a toast to French *joie de vivre,* and I in turn toasted their entrepreneurial spirit. We stood and applauded the impressive work of Sara and Eileen.

I remember, very clearly, thinking that I would never hold another workshop in France. It could never approach the glittering memory of this first one. It was the perfect event, and this was the perfect day.

The late-day sun cast shadows across the courtyard. Our new friends said farewell and disappeared through the gates. Eileen and I began bringing the tables back into the house. Sara started packing for a trip to Chinon in the Loire Valley. Eileen brought in the last of the cane chairs and set it down in the kitchen.

"I have to say something," she said, tired lines showing on her face. "Your daughter worked extremely hard to make this happen. I know you paid her, but you owe her more."

I nodded. I stacked up the dishes while Eileen loaded the glasses into the dishwasher. I knocked on Sara's door to say goodnight. Her train was scheduled to leave first thing in the morning.

"Dad, you weren't here," she said. "Mom did a massive amount of work this week. She's exhausted. Take her on a little trip. Say thank you."

I hugged her and stuck some extra cash in her pocket. A trip for Eileen was a wonderful idea. Maybe Lyon. Better yet, romantic Île de Ré, with its little white houses by the sea.

QUICHE AUX GIROLLES
Chanterelle Mushroom Quiche

Josianne, wife of Georges the contractor, can throw together
a superb spread with enviable confidence. When I asked her
the secret to her pastry crust she informed me that the pre-
rolled crusts available in French *supermarchés* are so good that
no one in France bothers making their own. Whether you
buy the crust or make it, this quiche is a wonderful vehicle
for the fragrant girolles mushrooms that abound in the village
markets every spring. The American equivalent, chanterelles,
can be a little pricey in the States, but they are so wonderfully
flavorful that even if you mix them with some less expensive
varieties of mushrooms, like oyster or shiitake, their flavor
will shine through. —*Sara*

Flour, for rolling crust
1 eight-ounce round pâte brisée
3 tablespoons unsalted butter
20 ounces chanterelle mushrooms, cleaned and sliced
    (about 4 cups)
3 tablespoons roughly chopped flat-leaf parsley
1 large clove garlic, minced
Salt and pepper to taste
2 large eggs
1 cup whole milk
1 cup crème fraîche

1. Heat oven to 400°F. Roll out pâte brisée on a floured surface to a 15-inch round. Lightly roll dough back up over pin and use it to drape over a 12-inch tarte tin. Press dough onto bottom and sides of tin. Roll pin over the top of tin to trim dough so it is flush with the tin. Chill in freezer 20 minutes.

2. Line the crust with foil or parchment; fill with dried beans or pie weight. Bake until sides of crust are set, about 15 minutes. Remove foil or parchment and beans. Continue to bake until bottom is set and golden, about 10 minutes longer. Set aside.

3. Melt butter in a large, high-sided skillet over medium heat. Add mushrooms, parsley, and garlic. Cook, stirring occasionally, until mushrooms are tender and fragrant, about 20 minutes. Season to taste with salt and pepper.

4. Reduce temperature to 350°F. In a large bowl whisk together eggs, milk, and crème fraîche. Add mushroom mixture and adjust seasoning with more salt if necessary. Pour custard and mushroom mixture into crust. Bake until custard has set, about 40 minutes. Let cool at least 10 minutes before serving

Serves 12

SAUMON À LA MOUTARDE
Lynn's Mustard Salmon

Years ago, my bubbly friend Lynn charmed this recipe from the fishmonger at Dean & Deluca, a high-end market in New York City. It's since become my go-to for impressing a large crowd with minimal effort and stress. The salmon is perforated with a skewer and then infused with olive oil, making it meltingly moist and tender when baked.

I was flattered when Susan and David Stuart, our dinner-hosting heroes, quickly added it to their repertoire.
—*Sara*

1 three-and-a-half pound salmon fillet,
   skinned and deboned
1/3 cup extra virgin olive oil
1/2 teaspoon kosher salt (optional)
1/4 cup Dijon mustard
1/4 cup country-style Dijon mustard
2 tablespoons small capers

1. Position oven rack under broiler. Heat to low-broil. Place salmon on a large baking tray. Use a skewer to liberally pierce salmon all over. Drizzle olive oil over fillet.

2. In a small bowl combine both mustards. Season salmon with salt, and spread evenly with mustard mixture. Sprinkle capers over the top.

3. Broil salmon until mustard is beginning to brown and salmon looks cooked through when center is pierced with a fork, 20–25 minutes. Delicious warm, room temperature, or chilled.

Serves 12 as a main course

SANGRIA BLANCHE À L'OLIVINO
Olivino's White Sangria

The owner of my local Brooklyn wine shop, Katrine, is both a Francophile and a pug owner. One day while gushing over pug pictures and French wines she shared with me this stellar idea for using Monbazillac, the famous dessert wine produced a few villages away from our house. This creates a sangria that is light and not too sweet—perfect for daytime quaffing. For a stronger, edgier sangria you can add a bit of brandy, cognac, or calvados. —*Sara*

3 bottles dry white wine
2 cups peach juice
375-ml bottle Monbazillac (or Beaumes de Venise)

3 cups thinly sliced citrus fruits
2 cups sliced peaches or other stone fruit
1 cup fresh or frozen raspberries
20 ounces plain carbonated water

Combine all ingredients except carbonated water in two large pitchers. Refrigerate 4 hours or overnight. Serve sangria over ice with a few pieces of fruit in each glass. Top each glass with a generous splash of carbonated water before serving.

Serves 8–10

☞ Photos and printable versions are at **www.beginningfrench.com**

Lesson 28

Jaqueline Piscine

I woke late the next morning. Eileen had been up for hours. She had taken Sara to the train station and returned to unload the dishwasher and scrub out the last of the pans.

When I finally wobbled into the kitchen, she was sitting at the table, a laptop open in front of her. The temperature in the room had dropped about twenty degrees. Eileen turned the computer around so I could see it. On the screen was a photo of a young woman wearing only a smile and a wet T-shirt. She was bending over the edge of a swimming pool with a vacuum hose in her hands. Cheery blue lettering on the T-shirt announced: *Jacqueline Piscine. Cool pools.*

"What's *this?*" Eileen said.

I peered at the screen. "That's Jacqueline. The girl who installed our carpets." I could feel my face reddening.

"I know who Jacqueline is. What about the email?"

I studied it closely. "I'm not sure. My French isn't that good."

"Really. It must have been good enough to invite her to lunch."

"Lunch?"

"Lunch. *Déjeuner.* When did you start sending kisses?"

"Kisses?"

"Stop repeating everything I say. Kisses. *Bisous.* Right here. *Bisou, bisou, bisou.* We'll skip the cliché that says you're old enough to be her father. You're old enough to be her *grand-*father."

"I have no idea what's going on," I said.

"I do." She slapped the laptop shut. "I'm tired. I'm more tired now than when we got here. If that's even possible. Sara and I worked for three weeks to give you this party, and I never heard those two little words."

"I love you?"

"That's three."

"Three?"

"Stop it!" she said. "Listen, your party was a huge success. Good for you. You worked hard. Sara's off on a little vacation of her own. She deserves it. And now *I* need a break." There was a suitcase by the door, and a pet carrier next to it.

"Where are you going?"

"Paris."

"Paris?"

Her eyes were agate. "I know you can't get both dogs home, so I'm taking Boodles with me."

"You're not coming back?"

"Nope. Not coming back. Oh, god, now *I'm* doing it."

"Doing what?

"Repeating everything. I'll see you in California." A horn sounded from outside the gates. "Would you please take my bags to the car? I'll get Boodles."

I thought, *Am I awake yet? Is this a bad dream?* I remember meeting Jacqueline at the bank. She was surprised to see me. She had a copy of my book. She must have used it to start a pool business. Did she really ask me to lunch? Is that what I agreed to? It's true, she kissed me on the cheek. Maybe both cheeks. *C'est normal en France, n'est-ce pas?*

We went out to Christine's car. The car, the sky, the fields, the house—seemed like a hand-tinted photo in all the wrong colors. Eileen got in, put down the window, and said, as if giving instructions to a baby sitter: "Take care of Bingo. Don't forget his eye drops. Walk him twice a day. And don't forget the toads."

"The toads?"

"In the pool. Every morning. If you have any questions, email me. Don't call. I won't answer." Christine accelerated down the dirt lane in a cloud of yellow dust.

"Thank you!" I shouted after the car. "T-H-A-N-K Y-O-U." Two little words. Too late.

Lesson 29

The Lady Vanishes

I WALKED BACK to the house. Bingo stood motionless in the kitchen. A look of panic filled his eyes. "That's right, Bingley, you and me. Bachelors together." I picked him up gently and sat down in the salon.

What had just happened? Only yesterday I was on top of Mt. Everest. Today I'm lying in the Mariana Trench. When the going gets tough, the tough make lists. I got up and went to my desk. I pulled out a sheet of paper and started writing.

TO DO
Walk and feed Bingo twice a day
Clean his eyes and ears
Allergy pills in peanut butter as needed
Apply his eye medicine twice a day
Shop for food, cook meals, do dishes (night markets?)
Make bed and vacuum floor
Wash and dry laundry
Sweep terrace, water pots

Pay bills
Clean pool once a week (Derek?)
Remove toads

I also had to continue returning emails, writing proposals, and working on my next book. It was a lot.

I looked at Bingo. "Did you ever have this kind of trouble with Boodles?" He cocked his head. He seemed to be parsing the sentence for key words—*walk, car, trick, treat.* Was that *Boodles* or *foodles?*

"Now I'm starting to lose it," I said. "I'm talking to a dog." Bingo heard the word *dog* and licked my chin.

I stared at the wall. I noticed the undulating surface as the light from the desk lamp raked across plaster-covered stones. Such a pretty house. With every trip we had tried to complete one big project and one or two smaller ones. I remembered how long it had taken to furnish the rooms. The brocantes, the big-box stores, the shopping excursions to Bordeaux.

I stared at the high ceiling of the salon, trying to guess the age of the thick wooden beams. How many couples had lived here before us? What were they like? Were they rich or poor? Did they have children? Did they have fights? Were they in love?

Enough of that. Don't think. Do.

"Come on, Bings." I headed into the laundry room. The dryer had been beeping every few minutes since Eileen left. I looked closely at the controls. They were all in French: *séchage, repasseuse, fer à repasser, séchage normal, air froid, infroissable-arrêt, vider réservoir.* The lights next to *infroissable-arrêt* and *vider réservoir* were on. I groaned. Bingo groaned. What does *vider réservoir* mean? Empty the reservoir? I took out the clothes and dumped them on the floor. The light stayed on. What about *infroissable-arrêt? Arrêt* means stop. But what about *infroissable?* Impossible? Impossible to stop? I shut the door. The whole cycle started over with *séchage.*

Bingo barked.

"You're right, Bings. It's a sign."

I poured a glass of rosé and sat down in the salon. Bingo followed and jumped into a big chair opposite mine. I gazed into the blackness of his face. He gazed back.

"You think it's my fault."

He said nothing.

"You think if I hadn't flirted with Jacqueline, Eileen would still be here."

He looked at me.

"I never invited Jacqueline to lunch. She must have invited *me* to lunch—in French—and I accidentally agreed. *I'm* the victim here. Do you think if I simply explained this to Eileen she might come home?"

He let out a king-size rebel yell. "W-r-a-a-a-o-o-a-a-h-r!"

"Yeah? You think it would work?"

"B-r-r-r-r-r-l," he said encouragingly.

"The only problem is, she won't talk to me. She said I could email her with questions, but no phone calls."

He put his head on his paws.

"I got it—I'll email her with a question: Can I call you?"

Bingo exhaled noisily.

"No, I guess not. What should I do?"

Silence.

"How about this. I'll find out where she's staying and send her a huge bouquet of flowers. Attached to the flowers will be a small card from *you* that says, 'I ruv you.' She'll be charmed, impressed. I'll send her an email about how much you miss her. I'll offer to set up a Skype call."

Bingo sat up in his chair.

"That's it! Thanks for your help, Bings, old boy. You're such a good listener! I know how much you miss her. I miss her, too."

Bingo looked at me sadly. Could he tell what I was thinking? Of course not. He always looks like that. He's a pug. It was time for his dinner. I'd wasted a whole hour talking to a dog.

I called Christine. "Push the button right above the orange button," she said. "And don't worry about Eileen. She just needs time to sort out her odds and sods."

"Do you know where she went?" I asked.

"Paris."

I hung up and prepared Bingo's dinner. Walked him. Fed him. Gave him a pill. Rubbed Vaseline on his nose. Changed his water and shook out his bed. I was exhausted, and this was only the first day. How many odds and sods did Eileen have?

A day's worth? A week's worth? A month's worth? More?

I reheated a container of leftover duck confit and potatoes Sarladaise and tried to eat. No appetite. I covered the food and stuck it back in the fridge. I went to bed early and lay there for hours before falling into a fitful sleep.

I had a dream that the kitchen was full of people. On the edge of the table was a ceramic pitcher that Eileen and I had purchased at a local brocante. I remember how excited we were to find it. The French blue of the pitcher matched the French blue of our shabby-chic table. In my dream we were using it for sunflowers.

I worried that someone might bump into it. I tried to move the vase to the center of the table, but instead I knocked it off the edge. I watched as it floated slowly downward toward the red clay tiles, where it cracked into a thousand pieces. Water flooded the kitchen floor, carrying limp yellow sunflowers in its wake.

Eileen stood in the doorway. She placed her hand over her mouth. I looked down at the broken pieces. The water and the flowers had disappeared, leaving only blue shards. There weren't a thousand pieces after all, just six or seven. They could be glued back together. I picked them up and set them on the table. Yet no matter how much I tried, I couldn't figure out how they fit together. A wave of sadness washed over me. I woke up.

When I went back to sleep, the dream started up again. The pieces wouldn't fit. They kept changing shapes. There were more of them. The dream repeated all night. I woke up, went back to sleep, and the pieces wouldn't fit.

The next morning I was more exhausted. I still had no idea of how to reach Eileen. I squinted at my to-do list. Bingo, laundry, watering, pool, pay the bills. I also had two conference calls, and an article to finish. I can be as brave as the next trooper, but this was too much for a platoon. It dawned on me that *this* might be my life, not the fantasy world of French food, wine tasting, and scintillating parties. How did Eileen keep up with all this work and still have time for herself? Maybe she didn't. Maybe that's why she left.

I have only two rules in life.

One, do unto others. It's not called the Golden Rule for nothing. Most of the world's successful religions are based on it.

Two, don't make Eileen mad. She has a short fuse. It burns slowly at first, then accelerates so quickly you don't have time to run. She's not being mean or selfish. Her explosions are always in the service of social justice. I remember the effect she had on that unsuspecting chef in Paris. And I'd bet good money he hasn't brandished a knife at anyone since.

Clearly, I had broken both rules at the same time. I wouldn't like it if I thought Eileen was seriously flirting with the pool man. Or the boulanger. Or the village doctor. But that's pretty much what I did to her. And now she's so angry she won't speak to me.

A marriage is a partnership. Everyone knows that. But what *is* a partnership? Is it just an agreement in which the work and the wealth are split down the middle? Or is it a relationship in which both partners contribute something meaningful? Listen with their whole hearts? Love first, ask questions later. Have each other's backs?

Eileen had my back when our business got in trouble. She had my back when I needed time to write a book and there was no money coming in. She had my back when I was so busy with client work I couldn't pick up Sara from school. Yet when she needed the tiniest bit of appreciation from me, a thank-you, I wasn't there for her. What kind of partnership is that?

I sat down at my computer to write her an email. Bingo jumped on my lap.

"I'm telling you, Bingley. This whole situation is *infroissable.*" I looked up *infroissable* on Google Translate. It said wrinkle. "Okay, the whole thing's wrinkled." Maybe that's it. I just need to iron it out.

"W-r-a-a-a-o-o-o-a-a-a-h-r!"

Lesson 30

Sécheresse

Cher Boodles,

*Aimes-tu Paris? Les frites sont bonnes? Tu me
manques beaucoup. Je voudrais parler sur Skype.
Peut-être demain?*

Ton petit ami,
Bingo

I hit send.

I wasn't sure if Bingo missed Boodles, but I missed Eileen.
And I knew Boodles wouldn't pass up a chance to appear on
Skype. It's been said that the only difference between humans
and the other animals is our ability to accessorize. If this is
true, Boodles must be human. She likes to dress up for videos
and photo sessions. The camera loves her. She'll turn her face
this way and that to show off her elegant flat profile.

More to the point, Boodles will keep Bingo's attention. I
can stick my face next to his and make my case to Eileen. The

flowers would have to wait until I knew where she was.

The phone rang. Could this be her already?

"Peter here. How's your house?"

"What do you mean, how's my house? Fine. How's yours?"

"Not so good. There's a long crack running down the wall of our lounge."

"Really?"

"It's the *sécheresse*. In the spring we had the most ungodly rain, followed by the most ungodly heat. It dried the soil and caused subsidence. Mind if I come over and take a look?"

Peter came into the house and walked from room to room. "Thought so," he said, standing in the salon with his head angled back. "Right there. Where the wall and the ceiling come together. They're starting to separate." He led me into the guest bedroom, ducking his head for the low doorway. "Here, too. See how the stones are pulling away from the beams? Eventually, this part of the ceiling will collapse."

I had thought I couldn't feel any worse. I was wrong. Eileen and I had cracks in our marriage and now we had cracks in our house. Our life was coming apart at the seams.

Peter waited. My insides were an anxious tangle of emotions. I couldn't think of a thing to say.

"Chris and I are going down to the *mairie*," he continued. "If enough people report problems, the mayor can declare an official *sécheresse*. Catastrophes are covered by home insurance."

Two days later, no call from Eileen. My plan had failed.

She didn't want to talk to me. She didn't even want to talk to Bingo. The crack in the salon wall seemed to get bigger by the second.

"If it's not one thing it's ten, right, Bingley?"

He placed a paw up on my knee. I moved my chair back and he leapt onto my lap. Did the floor just flex? I put Bingo down and stood where the chair had been resting. I bounced up and down. The floorboards creaked. Something snapped. I put Bingo down and called Derek on his mobile phone.

"Jan and I are just finishing a job in Monbazillac," he said. "We can be there in about thirty minutes."

Derek is the most practical person in the world. He claims no expertise in any subject, yet he's a problem-solver par excellence. He's humble, calm, and thoughtful in the face of adversity.

"You're having difficulties?" said Jan, parting the beads at the front door. Understatement of the year.

"Just a few," I said.

Derek went into the salon and bounced on the floor several times. He ran his hands through his hair. I excused myself to take a conference call in the kitchen, closing the door behind me.

A minute later there was a sickening crack. "Derek!" cried Jan. I dropped the phone. Derek was up to his knees in floorboards. Jan was trying to pull him out. The old planks had given way, and the more she pulled, the more the floor splintered.

"Don't move." I ran into the barn and got a heavy two by eight. I laid it across the floorboards in front of Derek. Jan and I stood on either end of it, supporting Derek by his elbows. He carefully extracted one foot, then the other from the splintery trap. There was a trickle of blood showing through his torn pant leg.

"Are you okay?" I said.

"I'm fine." He brushed off bits of debris from his clothing. "But this floor's a goner. Look at the wood. It must be a hundred years old." He went out to get a piece of plywood from the barn, came back and covered the hole.

"Listen, as long as I'm here I may as well check on the pool." Jan followed him out.

I went back to my conference call. By then the other callers had hung up.

Derek stuck his head through the beads. "Bad news," he said. "It looks like the pool might have a leak."

I put the phone down. "Derek," I said. "Look at me. Am I awake? First the wall, then the floor, now the pool. Are we both in the same bad dream?

"Sorry, mate. We're both awake."

On the morning of day four I took stock of the situation. Was there anything to celebrate? No. Now I needed a second list, an extraordinary to-do list.

Added to the structural issues (wall, floor, pool), there

were two smaller problems. First, I still hadn't finished my article. Second, we'd lost the clients we'd been wooing on the conference call. They told my colleagues that my sudden disappearance was not the main reason, merely a "contributing factor" in choosing another firm.

I pulled out a second sheet of paper and started writing.

TO DO (EXTRAORDINARY)
Deal with wall
Repair salon floor
Fix pool leak
Finish article
Apologize to team

I thought a little more, then added the most important item.

Get Eileen back

I moved that one to the top. I'm used to solving problems. I *enjoy* solving problems. My to-do lists can be several pages long. My calendar can have six or seven meetings a day. I can bring imagination to bear on intransigent problems and motivate people to work together constructively. That's my business. But this other business—the business of relationships—I often find baffling.

When I solve a business problem, it usually stays solved. I can cross it off the list. It doesn't crawl to its feet and track me down. Relationship problems are zombies. Just when you think you've killed one, it reappears right behind you, dragging its blood-soaked Ferragamos in slow-motion pursuit.

Which zombie am I dealing with? The flirting zombie? The workaholic zombie? The bad-listener zombie? The never-say-thank-you zombie? The whole living-dead community?

I sent another email to Eileen. "Miss you," I wrote. "Life here isn't the same. Hope you and Boodles are painting the town. Marty and Bingo."

Hours passed. No reply.

I glanced at the salon. The hole was still there, right by my desk in the corner of the room. If it's broke, sometimes it *does* need to be fixed. But for now I'd have to work in the kitchen. I sat at the table and went back to my article, "Ten Ways to Jumpstart Creativity."

"I hope it's good, Bings. I could use the advice."

The phone rang. Peter. "Georges is here. He can take a look at your house as soon as he finishes with ours. We'll meet you out front."

Georges stood on the road outside the house. He walked over to the corner and sighted down the wall. He walked to the other corner and did the same. Peter and I followed suit. We looked Georges.

"*Oh la la la la.*" He shook his head. "*Le mur tombe.*" *Tombe,* from *tomber,* to fall down. He kicked at some shards of plaster lying at the base of the wall. "*Le plâtre ne peut pas tenir.*" He said the plaster can't hold. My disaster-French was improving. The wall was bowing outward and popping off pieces of *plâtre*.

"*Et la solution?*" I asked.

"*La même,*" he said, nodding toward the barn. "*Enlever le mur de pierre par pierre, puis le reconstruire.*"

"Take it down stone by stone and rebuild it," Peter said. "Just like the barn."

Good lord.

I led Georges into the salon to look at the floor. He crouched down and lifted the edges of the wood next to the wall. Some of the floorboards had come off the foundation. That explained the accident with Derek. Was it possible that the floor and the wall were both caused by the *sécheresse?*

Georges said *au revoir* and got into his truck. Peter and I sat in the salon and talked for a good long time. When he finally got up to go, I had a new plan.

Lesson 31

The Train to Saint-Germain

THE CHIMES IN THE GARE ST. JEAN were followed by an announcement: *Votre attention, s'il vous plaît. Le TGV numéro 6224 départs 13 heures 18, partira voie 3.* I'd be in Paris by late afternoon.

Peter gave me the idea. All I had to do was access Find My Phone to see where Eileen was staying—or at least where my phone was staying. The GPS signal put her at the Hotel Saint-Germain de Pres in the sixth arrondissement.

"We'll take care of Bingo," he said.

The train was due to arrive in three hours, allowing me just enough time to formulate an apology. *C'est de ma faute,* I thought. *Tout est de ma faute.* It was my duty to put things right.

I gazed out the window at the wheat fields, now a golden blur. Beside me sat a white-haired man reading a copy of *Le Monde.* Across the table was a middle-aged woman with a young boy who was busy working on a puzzle. He might have been twelve. What would it be like to be twelve again, so full of energy and hidden promise? What will he do with his life?

What path will he choose? Will he find love?

The French word for foreigner is *étranger,* stranger. How strange it was to be on a train to Paris, asking the same questions at a much older age, feeling like a stranger even to myself. Such a specific moment out of all possible moments.

I opened my notebook and began to draw a diagram. What happens to people in a marriage? They start out in love. I drew a heart. They meet with the usual pressures of life. I drew a dollar sign, a baby bottle, a house, a clock. Then I drew a jagged starburst. Conflict. Maybe it starts when one person forgets to say thank you. Soon the other stops giving. Next come disrespect, withdrawal, and separation. I connected these with a tangle of arrows. My diagram looked like a giant hairball. How do you unravel a problem like this? I drew a giant question mark and circled it three times.

The white-haired gentleman looked over my shoulder. He put down his newspaper and leaned toward me. "You know," he said, tapping my notebook with his finger, "it is not so *compliqué.*" His accent sounded a little French and a little what—German? "Women do not need a picture. They are not so difficult. Marriage is a dance, *n'est-ce pas?*"

I looked at my diagram. Fred Astaire had just tripped Ginger Rogers, and she lay face down on the floor with a broken heel.

"Sometimes you lead. Sometimes you follow. But you must have the same rhythm. All women know this."

Rhythm, I informed him, was not my strong suit.

"Not only rhythm. You must have responsibility—sometimes for things you do not do. You must never let her fall."

I closed the book and looked out the window. The train was slowing as it entered the outskirts of Paris. My stomach churned and my head felt light. The train pulled into the gare and I reached for my overnight bag. I looked around for the word TAXI.

The Hotel Saint-Germain des Près turned out to be a nice establishment with traditional French furniture and flowered wall coverings. Just the kind of place Eileen would choose for Boodles. A uniformed man with a flashing smile held the door open for me. I showed my passport to the woman behind the counter and asked if my wife was a guest there.

"Oui, monsieur," she said, turning to look at the room keys, *"mais elle n'est pas ici."*

Eileen had probably taken Boodles for a walk. But where? Paris is a large place. I couldn't just roam around looking here and there. I left my bag with the concierge and went to an internet café. I looked up the location of my phone. Still at the hotel.

Think. Where would I take Boodles on a nice sunny afternoon? The Jardin du Luxembourg, *bien sûr.* Only a few blocks away. But even if they *were* there, what were my chances? The garden is over 50 acres. There must be a thousand people or more at any given time.

I stopped walking. Hadn't she said something about the Café de Flore? I'd just passed it five minutes ago. I turned around and hurried back. It was on the corner of Boulevard Saint-Germain and Rue Saint-Benoît, under a big white awning. There, at a small table on the far side, sat Eileen in one chair, sipping a kir, and Boodles, wearing a rhinestone collar, in the other. They'd been crossing items off Boodles's bucket list.

"Bonjour mesdames," I said nonchalantly, strolling up like Maurice Chevalier. "How nice to find two such elegant ladies enjoying the afternoon sun. May I join you?"

Eileen looked up. "Oh, you," she said. Boodles yawned.

"You were expecting...?" I pulled up a chair. I couldn't help notice how the Paris sunlight lit up the rim of her coppery hair.

"How did you find me?" she asked.

"You took my cell phone by accident. I used GPS. Listen, I need to talk to y—"

"You have to stop sending me flowers," she said. "It's embarassing. And expensive. I've been moving them into the hallway, and now the hotel wants me to pay for another room."

It was true that I'd ordered a large bouquet to be delivered every hour since the early morning. That made eight bouquets so far. But I was hoping for a better reception.

"I like my life here," she continued. "I sleep late every morning. I don't do the laundry. I don't do the dishes. The hotel cleans my room. Mike walks Boodles while I have breakfast."

"Mike?"

"Michel, the doorman."

I paused to take that in. The flashing smile. "Hey, I'm really sorry about the whole Jacqueline thing. It was all a big mistake."

"I don't care about Jacqueline. Do you really think I care about the machinations of a teenage pool queen? What I care about is respect."

"Before you say anything, I have a little speech." She straightened her posture and looked at me. Boodles did the same.

"I know I can be flirty," I said. "I don't usually think of myself that way, but, hey—if it quacks like a duck."

"I've never minded," she said. "Just another one of your char—"

"Wait, let me finish. I know that's not the problem. The real problem is that I don't say thank you. Two little words, remember? I don't even know where to begin to apologize for this."

"You don't have to—"

I held up my hand. "Our whole life long we've worked together to make something special. We've built a family. We've built a business. We've built a life. You inspired me to be more than I could ever be without you. You showed me a larger world of literature, history, theater, classical music."

"Have you submitted my name to the pope yet? Don't go

overboard. You helped me, too."

"And then you learned bookkeeping so that the little money I made would amount to something later on."

"And you know how much English majors love book-keeping."

"Yes. But imagine what would've happened if I had been doing the books. We'd still be paying off loans and living hand to mouth."

"So now we have a nice home in California and a charm-ing—if somewhat crumbling—cottage in France. We travel to interesting places and spend time with our wonderful daughter. On top of that, you've given me space to be creative and follow my passion. And how do I repay you? By taking everything as if it were free. *Thank you* doesn't begin to cover it. I should have been sending you bouquets every hour from the day we were married."

"Great, more flowers. Just what I need."

"What you need is a lot more appreciation. We've been lucky. We've followed our dreams. Sometimes we've succeed-ed, sometimes we've failed, but we've always had fun. It isn't fun without you. I need a crybaby do-over, a clean slate."

"I'm listening."

"First of all, you've washed your last dish this summer. From now on, when you come to France, you're on vacation. You deserve time to sightsee, read, write, catch up on your sleep."

"But I *like* to work."

"You can do it whenever you want, but in France you'll have to insist.

"Next," I said, "you should take a sabbatical. I'll cover for you. If you want to study French in Bordeaux, just go. If you want to join a garden tour in Cotswolds, go. It's time for you to follow *your* passions. You've earned it.

"Last, I promise never to take our life together for granted. Not just because of all the work you do. But because you're my best friend. My favorite teacher. My secret weapon."

"Now I'm a weapon? What—a Thompson sub-machine pop-gun?"

"A heat-seeking, heart-seeking, Joan-of-Arc missile. You're *formidable.* I want *you* to know that *I* know. Can I start by saying thank you?"

I took her hand. "Will you?"

"Will I what?"

"Forgive me? Finish our summer in France together?"

"Nice speech," she said. "I'm really touched by your thoughtfulness and effort. Of course I forgive you. But no. Sorry."

My head was pounding.

She said, "Now let *me* say something. I know I have a short fuse, but I always thought that I never held a grudge. Now I know I have a short fuse *and* I hold a grudge. And I'm holding one right now. Marty, I'm really, really tired."

"Isn't there anything I can do?"

"Please, leave me alone. Give me time to rest. I'll see you

in California."

I didn't dare tell her about the leaking pool, the hole in the floor, and the falling-down wall. I retrieved my bag from the hotel and took the 19:12 back to Le Rêve.

Lesson 32

Tour de France

THE WEEK BEFORE the big race, the Dordogne was swarming with cyclists. The Tour de France had inspired every guy with a bike to put on logo-spattered Spandex and hit the road. Hundreds of amateurs, in a one-time burst of energy, tested the route to see what the pros would be up against.

Stage 19 of the Tour would bring the riders from Marbourguet, down south in the Pays du Val d'Adour, up to Bergerac. In a *coup de chance,* the route passed through the nearby village of Monbazillac.

"As flat as it is, and as long as it is," said the announcer for the Tour, "there is one possible obstacle to a sprint on the final run—the Côte de Monbazillac." Here the road climbs slightly, a mere 64 meters, presenting one final challenge to the riders before they rushed down the hill into Bergerac. Any surprise in Monbazillac could split the race.

Monbazillac is a cute village by any standard. But it was cutified beyond recognition for the benefit of the cameras. Thousands of big, bright yellow flowers, handmade by locals from rolls of shiny vinyl, hung across the streets in all their plastic glory. For miles around, along the route and in the middle of the roundabouts, were festive displays of bicycles. Bicycles welded into towering sculptures. Bicycles painted in fluorescent colors of pink, orange, turquoise. Giant bicycles that towered over the traffic circles. Flocks of tiny bicycles frozen in space around electric poles. The detour signs had already been planted at key intersections, their messages covered in black tape, ready for unveiling on the day of the race.

It was now the morning before. Christine offered to prepare a *petit pique-nique* for the afternoon event. "The race will cheer you up," she said. It wouldn't, of course. But at least Bingo would have some fun, urging the riders forward with his famous rebel yell. W-r-a-a-a-o-o-o-a-a-a-h-r!

I busied myself with chores. Made the bed. Vacuumed the floors. Did the laundry. Washed the dishes. Fished the toads from the pool. The sun was high and hot at noon, the air slightly humid. I put Bingo in the sink and gave him a quick shampoo. When I toweled him off, he crashed through the beads onto the terrace, running in circles like a mad dog. "The zoomies," Eileen calls it. A pang of sadness hit me.

I made myself a déjeuner of semi-dried pork and Cabecou cheese on a baguette, washed it down with a small glass of rosé. Have a setback, have a belt—just like we always said. But I don't drink when I'm depressed. Not my style.

The gates to the courtyard groaned and the gravel crackled. A silhouette appeared in the beaded doorway. Boodles ran in, looking for Bingo.

"I'm back," said Eileen.

My mouth fell open. I rubbed my eyes. "Is it really you?"

"In the flesh. Who were you expecting, a hose-wielding pool goddess?

"But I—"

"I couldn't let you go to the Tour de France without your secret weapon."

"Secret weapon?"

"Listen. I was tired. I feel better now. All I needed was ten days of rest in a nice hotel. I'm refreshed, and ready to face the slings and arrows of country life."

I pulled her through the beads and wrapped my arms around her.

"Whoa, big boy. You'll warp my girlish figure."

I stepped back and took her in. She was dressed in a teal-green sundress I hadn't seen before. Her hair was shorter, copper curls framing her face. "It's just that I missed you so much."

"Show me the damage," she said.

"The damage?"

"You really have to stop repeating everything I say." She opened the door to the salon. The plywood still covered the hole in the floor. "We'll have to do something about *that*," she said.

"You know about it."

"Of course I know about it. Just because I wasn't talking to *you* doesn't mean I wasn't talking to anyone else. Christine told me."

"You're not upset?"

"What about? The house falling apart? Big deal. It's always falling apart. We've fixed it before and we'll fix it again. And again. On the positive side, at least the dishes are done."

"B-r-r-r-r-r-l." Bingo put his paws on Eileen's knee. She picked him up and scratched his chin.

I showed her my ever-growing to-do lists, now with the floor, the wall, and the disappearing pool.

"I don't suppose Jacqueline fixes leaks," she said.

"I'd be afraid to ask."

We spent the rest of the day catching up. I made our favorite Italian dinner, wild boar pasta with a white bean salad. For dessert I whipped up French-style sgroppini—a frappé of citron sorbet, champagne, crème épaisse, and vodka, with a mint leaf balanced on the foamy top.

The next morning we switched on the TV. The announcer huffed up an incline on a white bicycle, lapel mic clipped to his jersey. "This is Chris Boardman," he said, breathing heavily. "I'm in Monbazillac, 13.5 kilometers from the finish line of Stage 19. The riders are well behind me in Cahuzac-sur-Adour, where Peter Sagan has broken away from the *peloton*. Meanwhile, meteorologists are predicting a thunderstorm of Biblical proportions. It's due in Monbazillac around 17:00 hours, about the same time as the riders."

We looked at each other. What was he talking about? The sky was clear and blue. But by lunchtime it was tinged with an ominous yellow-gray.

"Better bring umbrellas," said Eileen. We had decided to leave at three. This would give us enough time to find a good spot and set out our picnic things. I was hoping to get close enough for some good action photos. How often does the Tour de France come through your own backyard?

At two o'clock it arrived. Just a few drops at first. Then a few more, heavier. And then it came down in sheets. Rain, rain, rain.

The phone rang.

"It's Peter. I checked the weather maps. It's not stopping. Chris and I plan to follow the race on TV. You're on your own, lads and lasses."

We stood at the window and watched the rain blow into the courtyard. The neighboring hamlet was now obscured by a veil of gray. The distant hills had vanished completely.

"Let's just skip it," I said. "Once we park our car, we're stuck. They won't let us leave until the race is over."

Eileen sighed. We made a pot of tea and turned on the TV. The riders were undaunted by the downpour. They kept up a steady pace, knocking off mile after mile.

"Here's an interesting fact," said the announcer. "Edmond Rostand, author of *Cyrano de Bergerac,* was the one who introduced the word *panache* to the world."

I turned to Eileen. "Did you know that?"

"Sure. The last word in the play. Too bad he didn't introduce the word *rebar.*" She nodded toward the collapsing stone wall. "That would have been useful."

Just before five, the peloton swarmed up the hill to Monbazillac. Sagan was out in front.

"Oh, *no!*" cried the announcer. "Sagan is down! It looks like his tires slipped on the slick surface as he rounded th—"

An earsplitting clap of thunder shook the house. The TV flickered and went dark. I looked at the salon wall. Still there. Another explosion, louder. We leapt from our chairs and ran to the window. A flash of lightning turned the barn stark white against a dark sky. Bingo and Boodles barked furiously. We rushed out to the terrace and stood under the overhang as a massive electrical discharge spidered its way across the blackness. A colossal clap of thunder ripped the air in two. We watched in stunned silence as flash after flash of electrical madness danced high above the horizon. The Tour de France could never compete with a spectacle like this. Right then there was no place on earth we'd rather be.

Some people have a deathly fear of thunder and lightning. *Tonnerre et foudre,* they call it in French. It strikes a primordial chord that can only be described as terrifying. For us, it's thrilling. In English we use the word *thunderstruck* to describe the moment we fall in love. In France, they say *coup de foudre,* struck by lightning.

The rumbling moved away to the east and I heard my cell phone ring. Peter again.

"We won!" he cried.

"Fantastic!" I said. "What did we win?"

"We got a letter from the mayor. The *sécheresse* is official! You'll get your new wall. You'll get your new floor."

I put the phone down and told Eileen the news. She shook her head, awed by the mysterious ways of bureaucracy. We went back outside to find that the storm had settled into a steady light rain. I took her by the hand walked her under the warm, soft showers. I put my arm around her waist. We danced to the rhythm of the rain.

"Look who learned to count," she said. "What happened to *you?*"

"I met an old man on a train," I replied. "I decided to be him before it was too late."

The clouds started to clear as the sky darkened. Constellations shimmered into view.

"You know what I like about you?" she said.

"Je ne sais pas? Quoi, ma chérie?"

"Your panache."

FRENCH SGROPPINI
Champagne and Sorbet Frappés

Many years ago Eileen and I took our first trip to Italy—the honeymoon we never had. We arrived at our Venice hotel on the wrong day, and were forced to grab the only room left on Lido. While dining at Trattoria Africa, around the corner, we noticed the locals ordering frothy drinks to accompany their blueberry cake desserts. We followed suit, and learned that the drinks were called sgroppini. Our scheduling mistake became a treasured memory.

Italians make their sgroppini with prosecco and lemon gelato. In France, we use champagne and citron sorbet, then add a splash of crème épaisse for a gelato-like creaminess. Be careful! These drinks are surprisingly potent. —*Marty*

3/4 cup chilled champagne (or prosecco)
1 cup lemon sorbet
1/4 cup vodka
1 tablespoon crème épaisse (or heavy cream)
Lemons slices or mint leaves as garnish

Place all the ingredients except the garnish into a blender. Mix on high for several seconds to get a thick, frothy consistency. Pour into two fountain glasses or large flutes. Top with either lemon slices or mint leaves.

Serves 2

Epilogue

IT WAS FRANCE, but it didn't have to be. Not for us. It could have been Italy. Or Spain. Or Morocco. It could have been the rocky coast of Dubrovnik, the temple-studded hills of Kyoto, the colorful streets of Istanbul—that city of minarets, bazaars, and contrasts. Any country different enough to shake us from our complacency. Any culture deep enough to keep us fascinated. Any language far enough from our own that it could force us to be beginners again.

But it was France, the country most beloved by travelers. When people hear we have a house there, they always ask the same questions: How often do you use it? Who takes care of it? How long have you had it?

Hidden beneath these questions are sometimes fanciful assumptions: You must be retired or independently wealthy to have a house in France. Your life is probably one long vacation with all those servants. It must be nice to inherit a luxurious chateau from your uncle. Well, people are entitled to their fantasies.

It was never our dream to live in luxury. It was always to travel broadly and experience deeply. We haven't journeyed from one five-star hotel to another, but from one five-star experience to another. It's true that we're rich—but our wealth is a wealth of learning, of friendship, of appreciation for other cultures. We were rich even when living on food stamps in our twenties. We were rich when we couldn't afford furniture for our house. We were rich in the recession when our business was losing money hand over fist.

"Sometimes I feel sorry for the one percent," said Eileen, setting aside the newspaper one morning.

"That's odd," I said. "Other people feel angry."

"No, seriously. Some people spend so much time and money building a massive wall around themselves that they never encounter real life."

"I guess we're safe, then. All we can afford is a small curb. Maybe some crime tape."

She was undeterred. "What *is* wealth, anyway? It's more than money, isn't it? Too many people with healthy bank accounts are actually broke. Their money keeps them from living richly."

"You're starting to channel Auntie Mame again: 'Live, live, live! Life is a banquet and most poor suckers are starving!'"

"Well?"

I had to agree. Money isn't wealth. It's only potential wealth. It might even be a barrier to wealth. Real wealth accrues when you invest in things that matter. Family, say, or your community. Your own education. Your ever-broadening view. This applies equally to the one percent and the other ninety-nine.

Owning a broken-down house in France is certainly not an example of wealth. But it could be a means to it. We've grown a lot in the time we've had it—learning a little bit of French *(un peu),* stretching our ability to navigate a different culture, and seeing our own culture through a different lens. It hasn't taken money so much as effort. It's the joyful struggle that creates the wealth.

A dream is only a wish, a light sketch of a possibility. Yet some dreams turn out to be the meaning of your life. What do you want your life to be? How big a world do you want to live in? How much do you want to discover who you'll become? You don't have to buy a house in a foreign country to address these questions. You don't need much more than a "travel attitude"—a curiosity about other people, other places, new experiences.

Admittedly, our dream was too big. We weren't satisfied to go to France. We weren't even satisfied to buy a house in France. We didn't just want to speak French. We wanted to *be* French. With every passing year our dream of learning another language seems more like a mirage than a dream, a goal receding endlessly into the distance. Yet we learned something even more important. We learned how to be better Americans, to become the best *étrangers* we could be. We learned to be thankful, to stand up and give a toast—*la vie est belle!*—to the loveliest country anyone could imagine.

———◆———

THE MAN MOVES through the house unplugging appliances. The stereo. The television. The DVD player he'd gotten replaced years ago on a rainy day when his French was nothing more than a few mispronounced words. Then the toaster. The tea kettle. The microwave. He unhooks the cooking utensils from the tool bar above the range and places them in a drawer. The knives in another drawer. He takes the candlesticks from the stolen table—it will always be the stolen table—and puts them in the pine confiture next to the cans of cassoulet. He looks around at the bare kitchen.

The woman packs up the bathroom. She wishes she could pack up the night sky. The rhythm of the vineyard. The pleasant chatter of the marketplace. Pack them up and bring them home. She places the bathroom items back into their baskets. She brings in the tall tin lanterns from the terrace. The wicker chairs. The cushions for the chaises longues. She folds the bed clothing and rolls up the cotton placemats, storing them high in the laundry room cabinet.

Together they swing the big blue shutters closed, bolting them tight from the inside. First the shutters for the French doors in the salon. Then the ones for the terrace and the garden. The couple feels the familiar twisting in their stomachs as they survey the dim rooms that will stay empty for months to come.

"I think I'm ready to go back," says the man.

"Me too," says the woman.

But neither means it. They turn the iron key in the kitchen door lock. They carry the luggage out to the car. The dogs jump in, ready for their next adventure. He closes the gates to the courtyard and the view. She puts her arm around his waist and turns him to face the sign on the wall. *La Rêve.* The dream, misspelled.

They smile.

He walks over to the wall and gives it a pat. He whispers softly, *"Merci."*

Acknowledgments

WE SINCERELY THANK our early readers for their invaluable feedback during the writing process. First and foremost, we'd like to thank our friends Susan and David Stuart, Christine and Peter Johnson, and Cris and Gordon Mortensen—all of whom appear in the book—for their wholehearted encouragement and support.

We also thank Irene Hoffman, Debra Simon, Forrest Smith, and Faith Gasparrini, as well as family members Francele Beener, Gillian Taylor, Peter Neumeier, Ellyn Lennon, Joe Lennon, and Marty's mother Lorna, for their comments and suggestions during the early stages.

Francele Beener's book club provided a clear view of what was working and not working in the story, which was immensely helpful. Thanks to Corinne Dawson, Ronda Gottlieb, Pat Knutson, Jerrie Newman, Teresa Olmos, Carole Paul, Lynn Poltere, Helen Tanquary, Mary C. White, and Sally Yussam.

We're grateful to our editor Elizabeth Welch for combing out the errors and tightening up our prose, and to colleagues Nikki McDonald, Esmond Harmsworth, Mark McGuinness, and Meg Thompson for their professional insights.

Our gratitude also goes to Cya Nelson Drew for designing and maintaining the beginningfrench.com website, and to Nicki Gauthier for managing the book's online marketing and distribution.

Sara thanks her friends Lynn Rutledge and Katrine Pollari (and Katrine's pug Olive) for sharing their excellent recipes.

Boodles and Bingo would like to thank Pat Rhode of Pets in Need Canine College for guiding them down the road to obedience and agility, and the wonderful vets and staff at San Roque Pet Hospital for filling out their travel documents every year. And a special shout-out to Tonya Jensen, a pug's best friend.

Un grand merci to our French-speaking advisers, Clara Carrere, Alain Calle, and Judy Flanagan, for vetting all the French passages. Clara, from nearby Monbazillac, sat down in our kitchen and went through the whole book in three hours, giggling and correcting our French as she went. Alain and his wife Andrea found even more errors, patiently explaining that nouns and their adjectives must agree—a concept which at times has eluded us.

We offer our heartfelt gratitude to our neighbors in the village, our *chers voisins,* who have welcomed us into their lives as honorary French. *Vous êtes très, très gentil.*

Glossary

*Note: French words can have different meanings in different contexts.
We've defined these by how they're used in the book.*

A

accoutrement	kit used for a specific activity
ah, mignon!	ah, cutie!
aimes-tu Paris?	do you like Paris?
air froid	cold air
à la	in the style of
allez	you go
allez au poissonier	you go to the fishmonger
allons-y	let's go
alors	so
Américains	Americans
appareil	appliance
appellation	official wine-growing area
Aquitaine	a region in southwest France
asseyez-vous	you sit down
aujourd'hui	today
au revoir	goodbye
avez-vous choisi?	have you chosen?
avez-vous d'autres?	do you have others?

B

baba au rhum	small cake with rum and chantilly
baguette	long, narrow loaf of French bread
barquette	container
bastide	medieval fortified town
beaucoup	very much
Béchamel	sauce made from butter, flour, and milk
belle	beautiful, pretty
Belles de nuit	fragrant, night-blooming plant
Bergerac sec	dry white wine of Bergerac
bien sûr	of course
bisous	kisses
bonjour	good day; hello
bonsoir	good evening
bonsoir à tous	good evening, everyone
boulanger	baker
boules	bowling game, also called *petanque*
BOUM!	BOOM!
brocante	flea market

C

cabécou	soft goat cheese from the Midi-Pyrénées
caillou	pebble
calcaire	limestone
cannage	caning
carte de visite	business card; calling card
cauchemar	nightmare
ça va?	how's it going?
ça va bien	it's going well
ce n'est pas de ta faute	it's not your fault [familiar]
centre-ville	city center

c'est à vous	it's to you; your turn
c'est de ma faute	it's my fault
c'est normal	it's normal
c'est tout?	is that all?
c'est une problème	it's a problem
chaise	chair
chaise longue	long chair
chambre	room; chamber
chantilly	sweet, light whipped cream
charlotte	sponge cake made in a mold
chemin rural	country road
chérie	sweetheart
Christophe Maé	French pop star
citron sorbet	lemon sherbet
cochonnet	piglet, or marker ball in boules
cocktail de la maison	special house cocktail
cocotte	casserole
combien pour…?	how much for…?
compliqué	complicated
confit de canard	preserved duck meat
coup de chance	stroke of luck
coup de foudre	stroke of lightning; love at first sight
crème de cassis	liqueur made from blackcurrants
crème fraîche	light sour cream
crème épaisse	heavy cream

D

d'abord…	firstly…
d'accord?	agreed?
déjeuner	lunch
département	an administrative division of France

Glossary

derrière	behind
desolé	orry
devis	cost estimate
dommage	too bad
Dordogne	a *département* in the Aquitaine

E

eau de vie	homemade liquor; moonshine
en bas	below
enchanté	nice to meet you; enchanted
*entrée*starter	dish
escargots	snails
escargots en coquille	snails in their shells
esprit de corps	group spirit; morale
étranger	stranger; foreigner
étudiant	student
et vous?	and you?
exactement	exactly
excusez moi	excuse me

F

fatigué	tired
faute	fault
fer à repasser	clothes iron
fête	celebration
filet de Saint-Pierre pôele	pan-fried whitefish
foie gras	fattened goose liver
formidable	wonderful
formule	all-inclusive meal; formula
frappé	slushy drink
fromager	cheesemonger

G

gallette	flat, round cake
garder vos bagages	watch our bags
garçon	boy
gâteau	cake
girolles	golden chanterelle mushrooms
gouffre	deep abyss
grand cauchemar	big nightmare
grand pichet de vin rouge	large pitcher of red wine
grange	barn
gris-bleu	gray-blue
grotte	cave

H

haute cuisine	high-quality cooking
heure	hour
homards	lobsters
hypermarché	hypermarket; superstore

I

ici	here
Île de Ré	island off the west coast of France
ils sont partis	they left
immédiatement	immediately
imposteurs	imposters
infroissable-arret	wrinkle-stop
invités d'honneur	guests of honor

J

j'ai terminé	I have finished
jamais	never

jambon sec	dry-cured ham
je ne comprends pas	I don't understand
je ne sais pas	I don't know
je ne sais quoi	I don't know what
je sais	I know
je sais pas	I don't know [slang version]
je suis désolé	I'm sorry
je suis petite	I'm small
je suis prêt	I'm ready
je vais tirer l'autre	I'll pull the other
joie de vivre	joy of life
jolie	nice; pretty
je m'appelle…	I call myself…
je vais te reveiller domain matin	I'll wake you in the morning
je voudrais parler sur Skype	I would like to talk on Skype
je voudrais retirer…	I would like to withdraw…
je vous présent…	I present to you…

K
Kir	white wine and *crème de cassis*

L
la machine	portable credit-card machine
langoustine	small Norwegian lobster
la vie est belle	life is beautiful
Leclerc	French hypermarket chain
les Américains	the Americans
les frites sont bonnes?	are the fries good?
Lot-et-Garonne	a *département* in the Aquitaine

M

mademoiselle	girl; unmarried woman
ma faute	my fault
magret	breast meat of the Moulard duck
mairie	mayor's office
mais elle n'est pas ici	but she's not here
mais oui	of course
maison à vendre	house for sale
maison de charme	charming house
mal de tête	headache
mangeoire	manger; feed trough
ma petite	my little girl
marche	it operates
marché bio	organic market
marché nocturne	night market; evening *fête*
marche pas	it doesn't operate
marquéz vos fruit	mark your fruit
meilleur	better
mélange	mixture
merci	thank you
merci beaucoup	thanks a lot
merde, pas la!	shit, not there!
mesdames	ladies
mes parents	my parents
messieurs	gentlemen
mesurer	to measure
Midi-Pyrénées	a region in southern France
moi, je suis le professeur	me, I'm the professor
moules et frites	mussels and fries
monsieur	sir, mister
mystère et boule de gomme	mystery and bubblegum

Glossary

N

naturellement	naturally
négligée	a woman's light dressing gown
n'est pas?	is it not?
nous avons bien mangé	we have eaten well

O

oh la la!	oh no!
oop-la!	heave-ho!
ouais	yeah
ou sont les homards?	where are the lobsters?
oui	yes
oui, ma fille?	yes, daughter?

P

panache	flamboyant style; a large plume
parlez-vous anglais?	do you speak English?
pas la	not there
pas mal	not bad
pas nécessaire	not necessary
pâté	paste of ground meat and fat
pâté en croûte	*pâté* baked in a crust
pâtisserie	pastry; pastry shop
pavé de saumon d'ecosse	slab of Scottish salmon
Pecharmant	Bergerac red-wine appellation
peinture	paint; painting
peloton	pack of cyclists
petanque	bowling, also called *boules*
petit, petite	small
petite pique-nique	little picnic
peut-être demain?	maybe tomorrow?

pichet	pitcher, carafe
pierre	stone
piscine	pool
plancher	floor
plâtre	plaster
poissonier	fishmonger
premiere étage	first floor (one floor up from ground)
pressé	hurry
probléme	problem
Provence	a region in southern France
putain	whore

Q

quel dommage	what a pity
quelle catastrophe	what a disaster
quelle grand chambre…	what a big room (you have)…
quelle est le remède?	what's the remedy?
quel tapis voulez-vous?	which carpet do you want?
qu'est-ce qui se passe?	what's going on?

R

racines	roots
reconstruire	to rebuild
recoucher	to lie down again
regarder	to watch
reméde	remedy
remplacer	to replace
repasseuse	ironer
rêve	dream
Rhône-Alpes	a region in southeast France
ris de veau	sweetbreads

Glossary

S

sais pas	dunno; *je ne sais pas*
salle des fêtes	banquet hall
salle polyvalente	multipurpose hall
sandales	sandals
santé!	(to your) health!
savoir-faire	know-how; adaptability
SCI	Société Civile Immobilière
séchage	drying
séchage normal	normal drying
sécheresse	drought
serviette de plage	beach towel
shabby chic	a rustic French style
s'il te plaît	please [familiar]
s'il vous plaît	please [formal]
soufflé glacé aux agrumes	citrus iced soufflé
soupçon	small amount; a suspicion
supermarché	supermarket

T

tarte au citron	lemon tart
terroir	unique farming environment
TGV	Train à Grande Vitesse; fast train
tonnere et foudre	thunder and lightning
ton petit ami	your boyfriend
tournesols	sunflowers
tout de suite	right now
très bien	very well
très difficile	very difficult
très jolie	very pretty
très, très belle	very, very beautiful

truffe	truffle
tu	you [familiar]
tuiles	tiles
tu es très, très fatigue	you're very, very tired
tu es un bon garçon	you're a good son
tu me manques beaucoup	I miss you very much
tutoyer	to address as *tu* [familiar]

U

un peu	a little
une phase	one phase
un système triphasé	a three-phase system

V

vider (le) reservoir	empty the tank
vie	life
vin rouge	red wine
voilà	there you have it
voisin	neighbor
votre voiture est trop petite	your car is too small
vous êtes les étudiants	you are the students
vous êtes un rock star	you're a rock star
vous-avez choisi?	have you chosen?
vous-avez un problème?	do you have a problem?
vous tirez une extrémité	you pull one end